60+
bush foods
and recipes

BUSH TUKKA GUIDE

2nd Edition

Samantha Martin

Hardie Grant
EXPLORE

First edition published by Explore Australia/Hardie Grant Travel in 2014 where full acknowledgements for individual contributions appear.

This second edition published in 2023 by Hardie Grant Explore, an imprint of Hardie Grant Publishing.

Hardie Grant Explore (Melbourne)
Wurundjeri Country
Building 1, 658 Church Street
Richmond, Victoria 3121

Hardie Grant Explore (Sydney)
Gadigal Country
Level 7, 45 Jones Street
Ultimo, NSW 2007

www.hardiegrant.com/au/explore

All rights reserved. No part of this publication may be reproduced, stored in a retrieval system or transmitted in any form by any means, electronic, mechanical, photocopying, recording or otherwise, without the prior written permission of the publishers and copyright holders.

The moral rights of the author have been asserted.

Copyright text, photography and artwork © Samantha Martin 2023
Copyright concept, maps and design © Hardie Grant Publishing 2023

The maps in this publication incorporate data © Commonwealth of Australia (Geoscience Australia), 2006. Geoscience Australia has not evaluated the data as altered and incorporated within this publication, and therefore gives no warranty regarding accuracy, completeness, currency or suitability for any particular purpose.

A catalogue record for this book is available from the National Library of Australia

Hardie Grant acknowledges the Traditional Owners of the Country on which we work, the Wurundjeri People of the Kulin Nation and the Gadigal People of the Eora Nation, and recognises their continuing connection to the land, waters and culture. We pay our respects to their Elders past and present.

For all relevant publications, Hardie Grant Explore commissions a First Nations consultant to review relevant content and provide feedback to ensure suitable language and information is included in the final book. Hardie Grant Explore also includes traditional place names and acknowledges Traditional Owners, where possible, in both the text and mapping for their publications.

Bush Tukka Guide 2nd edition
ISBN 9781741178272

10 9 8 7 6 5 4 3 2 1

Publisher
Melissa Kayser
Project editor
Amanda Louey
Editor
Ella Woods
Proofreader
Susan Keogh
First Nations consultant
Jamil Tye, Yorta Yorta
Cartographer
Emily Maffei
Design
Little Rocket Creative Agency
Typesetting
Kerry Cooke
Index
Max McMaster
Production coordinator
Simone Wall

Colour reproduction by Splitting Image Colour Studio

Printed and bound in China by LEO Paper Products LTD.

The paper this book is printed on is certified against the Forest Stewardship Council® Standards and other sources. FSC® promotes environmentally responsible, socially beneficial and economically viable management of the world's forests.

Disclaimer: While every care is taken to ensure the accuracy of the data within this product, the owners of the data (including the state, territory and Commonwealth governments of Australia) do not make any representations or warranties about its accuracy, reliability, completeness or suitability for any particular purpose and, to the extent permitted by law, the owners of the data disclaim all responsibility and all liability (including without limitation, liability in negligence) for all expenses, losses, damages (including indirect or consequential damages) and costs which might be incurred as a result of the data being inaccurate or incomplete in any way and for any reason.

Publisher's Disclaimers: The publisher cannot accept responsibility for any errors or omissions. The representation on the maps of any road or track is not necessarily evidence of public right of way. The publisher cannot be held responsible for any injury, loss or damage incurred during travel. It is vital to research any proposed trip thoroughly and seek the advice of relevant state and travel organisations before you leave.

Publisher's Note: Every effort has been made to ensure that the information in this book is accurate at the time of going to press. The publisher welcomes information and suggestions for correction or improvement.

Contents

Introduction

Acknowledgement

I, as an Aboriginal woman, would like to acknowledge and express my utmost respect for all the traditional lands on which this book is distributed to and read.

I wish to acknowledge the incredible people who have generously provided their language names to enrich the content provided in this little book. As we all know, some of our tribes around Australia are working to revitalise their languages; I feel that the *Bush Tukka Guide* is another way to preserve and share knowledge for generations to come.

I would also like to give a shout out to all the Elders and storytellers out there who are working to provide platforms for our cultural heritage to be shared and appreciated.

And finally, I would like to express my gratitude to the person who has purchased and is reading my book. May you find comfort in knowing you are taking part in the preservation, and passing on, of important knowledge from our rich, and the oldest living, culture on this planet. I thank you for your support.

About the author

Samantha Martin is a descendent of the Jaru from the East Kimberley region of Western Australia. She was born into a long line of traditional hunters and gatherers, and had the opportunity to learn from her family how to eat off the land and surrounding waters. These experiences have translated into a career sharing her knowledge of bush foods and survival skills, and promoting the health and wellbeing benefits of living off the land. The first edition of *Bush Tukka Guide* was published in 2014, since then Samantha has only continued to extend her reach as the Bush Tukka Woman.

Samantha now offers her services around Australia and all over the world. She hopes to continue inspiring people to explore the rich and diverse bush tukka and all it has to offer, and wants people to have fun doing it!

In honour of the first edition

While writing the first edition in 2013, I had a range of emotions flooding through me. I felt a sense of honour, but also a tremendous feeling of doubt came over me. I kept telling myself it was extremely important to complete the book, as it would add to the collection of cultural records, kept for future generations to come.

My Aboriginal name is Nyadbi; I am a descendent of the Jaru People from the East Kimberley region of Western Australia. Being Aboriginal plays an important role in my life story, including my love of bush tukka. It was obvious to me when I was just nine years old. My mother, Nancy Martin, was teaching me the value of bush tukka by acknowledging the change in seasons, what parts of plants and animals to eat and what parts not to eat.

I remember watching my mother and observing how much confidence and knowledge she had and that everything she was teaching me included other lessons, from the smallest thing of her showing me the shape of the leaves to the bark of the trees, how to track a goanna, track native bees to their hives and how to dig for yams. She told me to memorise all the information as one day it will come in handy; well, she was right! She explained that there are a lot of plants and animals that are poisonous and told me about the vigorous process our ancestors undertook before they ate a certain plant or animal to ensure all the toxins had been released from it first.

In the past, bush tukka has not received the respect it deserved. It was more of a novelty, despite the evidence of how healthy our people were before the invasion of western culture. You just have to look back through the archives to see the healthy physique that our ancestors embodied.

The last 200-plus years have seen our rich cultures deeply impacted, along with the health, knowledge and wellbeing of many of our people.

I am now witnessing widespread health problems in our communities due to the lack of knowledge, understanding, motivation and accessibility to healthy foods; my people are becoming very unwell with chronic diseases. This has a lot to do with not eating healthy, but also, I believe, due to not eating off the lands and waters as our ancestors did.

If I can inspire or motivate one person, I will feel I am making a difference. If I can share knowledge, to help preserve it for our future generations, I feel I am making a difference.

These books I'm publishing through Hardie Grant are my pride and joy – they have manifested from a dream of becoming an author, despite not being able to read or write until the age of 15. When I was told I was not good enough or worthy enough, I realised the importance of fighting for an education. I knew I needed this to become a voice for my ancestors, the unforgotten voice.

So, I share with you my passion to educate the world about my rich and wonderful culture and hope to inspire everyone to introduce bush tukka into their lives!

Happy hunting and gathering.

Love from,

The Bush Tukka Woman

Teachings from my ancestors

SHARED KNOWLEDGE

Australia is a unique and diverse country in every way – in history, culture, geography and climate. The knowledge about this great country that was shared with me by Aboriginal Elders is the richest knowledge I could ever wish for.

The Australian bush is home to a lot of edible and poisonous plants and wildlife. To identify edible plants in different areas around Australia is not that easy, but it is a good survival technique to have. To some people all trees and all shrubs look the same. Those who know what to look for, however, can identify what a plant is just by looking at the texture of

its bark, the colour and shape of its leaves, and the flowers that grow on that plant.

It is also helpful to know about the diverse changes in the landscape, where these plants grow best and what climates they thrive on. Aboriginal People carefully observed the environments they lived in. Some flora and fauna can only be found in certain parts of Australia. As for the fauna of our country, the witchetty grubs, for example, are predominantly found in central Australia and the freshwater eel is predominantly found in the waters along the east coast.

INDIGENOUS BACKGROUND KNOWLEDGE

Aboriginal People have survived and lived off this land for tens of thousands of years and have learned how to respect and acknowledge the land and the animals. Prior to colonisation, there were well over seven hundred different Aboriginal language groups sharing this country. Each clan had its own hunting tools, hunting and gathering techniques, Dreaming stories, language, and spiritual rituals. Each clan respected each other's boundaries and would on many occasions seek right of passage to trade tools, traditional foods, and sometimes women; this was one way of ruling out inbreeding within clans.

To me, the clan is an important unit in Aboriginal society. A clan is a group of about 40–50 people with common totems. It consists of groups of extended families. Generally, men born into the clan remain in the clan territory. This is called a patrilineal group, but everyone in the clan knew their own roles in keeping a peaceful and balanced family, from the men's responsibilities of hunting larger animals like kangaroo, emu and bustard birds, to the women and younger men's responsibilities of hunting the small animals such as goanna,

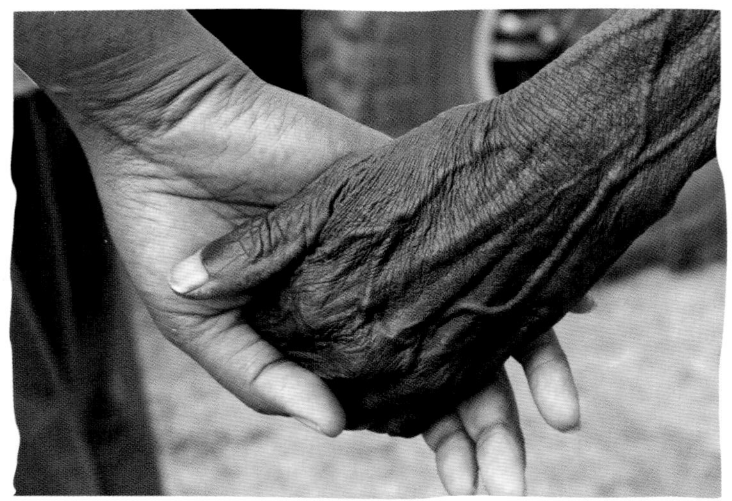

small rock wallabies, fish and echidnas. The women had other responsibilities as well, such as gathering bush berries, plums, bush medicines, and looking after the children and the Elders.

My ancestors knew how and where to hunt for food and never took anything more than they needed. What they killed they ate; they never let anything go to waste. They used the teeth, bones, hide, sinew, and feathers for making tools, costumes or weaponry. They also gave reverence to the life of the animals they killed, to take on the strength or the speed of that animal. But if the animal was someone's totem, that person was not allowed to eat it and, therefore, they did not kill or harm it.

SPIRITUAL TOTEMS

Most Aboriginal People will be given a totem. This means that they take on the spirituality of the animal, plant or other object believed to be ancestrally related to them. Totems can

be represented through nature in the form of a large rock, tree, hill, river, or other landform. A lot of Aboriginal art is connected with the imagery of the artists' totems.

WATER

Australia is one of the driest lands in the world, but the Aboriginal nomads knew exactly where to find water. They knew how to read the signs to follow a flock of birds flying by, which would lead them to waterholes. They knew the underground bores and springs which they could use as reliable sources of water; sometimes they would cover the holes up with a huge rock or sticks and leaves to keep the animals from drinking and contaminating the water.

PLANTS

The high diversity of Australia's flora includes large numbers of species which are ecologically significant, such as acacia, eucalyptus, melaleuca and grevillea. Acacias tend to dominate in drier inland parts of Australia, while eucalypts dominate in wetter parts.

Australian vegetation also plays an important part in the ecosystem and can be a great reference for Aboriginal People, indicating where they should look for bush tukka. In the northern part of Australia mangroves, savannah and tropical rainforests offer a supermarket of bush tukka. Aboriginal People in these areas, and other areas throughout Australia, relied heavily on the life cycle and the mating season of plants and animals which affected their survival in the Australian outback.

ANIMALS

In Australia there are more than 378 species of mammals, 828 species of birds, 300 species of lizards, 140 species of snakes and two species of crocodiles. Of the mammals, almost half are marsupials. The rest are either placental mammals or monotremes, which are mammals that lay eggs instead of giving birth to live young like marsupials, and placental mammals.

Among Australia's best known animals are the kangaroo, echidna and emu.

Our land, our Country

For thousands of years Aboriginal People have learned how to adapt and survive in the diverse and sometimes inhospitable environments found across the vast Australian landscape, learning the simplest but most important survival skills, like knowing how to find water and food in the driest and most desolate lands. They had to learn how best to hunt wild animals with the few tools they had or those they made from the natural resources that were accessible to them. They learned that not everything was edible and that some fruits, berries and nuts were highly toxic, but also that, with time and a long, drawn-out process, some of those fruits, berries and nuts became edible and could be used as an important staple of their diet. Today, Aboriginal People are still taught from an early age how to read the landscape; we are shown how to look for signs which show us when, where and how to find water and bush tukka.

The pure connection that an Aboriginal person has to this land is profoundly unique. When Aboriginal People are talking about our 'Country', what we are referring to is the land which our ancestors have inhabited for thousands of years; the same land we were born in, and the creeks, rivers and valleys in which we hunt and gather and celebrate important life events; where an unseen and unheard vibration runs deep through the land that connects us to a songline that we feel when we are born.

This feeling is a knowing and a bond we have to our mother's, father's, grandmother's and grandfather's land. It spreads throughout our veins like the very blood that runs through them. We dream about our land. We miss our land when we are away from it. And we feel we have a custodian's responsibility to protect and cherish our land, its stories and its existence as it has passed from one generation to the next for over 50,000 years.

The early European explorers found it almost impossible to survive in this land. Unsure of what foods could be eaten, they were reluctant to accept any foods generously shared by the local Aboriginal tribes, thinking it would bring ill health because it was foreign to them. Most of the first Europeans perished from starvation and hunger. But this land is abundant with fresh water and bush tukka, and with a little awareness and education it can be an enjoyable experience to look for, and find, bush tukka growing in its natural environments.

OUR LANDSCAPE

One of the most important survival skills to have is an understanding of the different environments in Australia. The landscape changes dramatically and plays an important part within the Indigenous culture. To recognise the changes in the landscape is to identify the distinct meaning and relevance of each landscape and what foods and resources are available. The southern half of Australia has a different landscape to the northern tropics of Australia. Southern Australia features a more Mediterranean climate and arid coastline with cold wet winters and hot dry summers. Most of Australia's northern tropical regions contain areas of mangrove swamps, rainforest, woodland, grassland and desert.

DESERT PEOPLE

The desert people of Australia are among the greatest hunters and gatherers. Having the skills, knowledge and understanding of where to find food and water in the desert is absolutely extraordinary. To a western person nothing grows in the desert because it's hot and has no life; there appears to be no food in the desert. They see nothing but red, hot sand and small, spindly shrubs. To the desert people, finding bush tukka is as easy as shopping in a supermarket: they know how to identify where they can find an underground spring, where to dig for wild yams, and how to find honey ants, witchetty grubs, echidnas and sand goannas. Growing up in the desert is harsh. Dealing with the heat is difficult and exhausting. The climate changes from extreme heat during the day to freezing temperatures at night.

Desert people rely heavily on their traditional practices of living off the land, but the introduction of four-wheel-drives makes it easier to get around the desert, allowing these desert people to travel across their Country more quickly than in the past. Desert people have great Dreaming stories of their Country. They depict stories of hunting and gathering through their traditional dance and extraordinary, vibrant artwork. This shows how important it is for them to teach younger generations about what they eat off their lands and how they survive.

RAINFOREST PEOPLE

Rainforest people are custodians of the forests. They have lived amongst some of the oldest living trees on our planet. Learning to survive in damp, cool, wet terrains, they have adapted to their thick, lush green surroundings. With fresh waterways readily accessible, they learned different methods of how to trap fish, freshwater prawns, freshwater eels and freshwater turtles, which provided them with the rich proteins and minerals they needed to be strong and healthy. The men and women would both participate in catching freshwater prawns by throwing handful of leaves from small waterholes (where the prawns live) onto the banks and grabbing the prawns before they scurried back into the water. They also used a certain plant, known as foam bark tree (*Jagera pseudorhus*) to stun fish. They crushed the leaves, put them in their dilly bags and soaked the leaves in still waterholes. This takes the oxygen out of the water and the fish would float to the surface where the rainforest people would gather them (the poison did not harm humans). The rainforest people also delighted in hunting scrub hens and collecting their eggs from their nesting mounds; they made nets to capture the scrub hens by using strong fibres obtained from the inner bark of particular fig trees.

They also gathered and ate wild berries, plums, roots, seeds, nuts and yams when they were in season and only took what they needed.

Rainforest people were very clever during the wet seasons. During this time they moved towards drier environments to escape the wet, damp and cold landscape which became difficult to hunt food in. They would return to the rainforest in the dry season when they needed to cool down from the scorching heat.

FRESHWATER PEOPLE

Freshwater people live inland from the coast, surrounded by vast lands. They rely on freshwater wetlands, swamps, rivers, creeks, waterholes and billabongs to catch many species of fish, freshwater turtles, freshwater eels and freshwater prawns. The freshwater people have a deep spiritual and cultural connection to these waterholes. Many tribes around Australia share in the common Dreaming stories of the rainbow serpent, the creator of the rivers and waterholes. The rainforest people believe that the waterholes hold a powerful spirit, which sleeps at the bottom of the waterholes and should be respected and not disturbed.

Living by waterholes like rivers, creeks and billabongs offers a protected and peaceful environment for the tribes. They can fish on a daily basis and gather under the cool, shaded paperbark and eucalyptus trees. The women and children also spend time swimming and collecting freshwater mussels from the banks and freshwater prawns from the rivers. But people from northern Australia also understood that setting up their camps by waterholes also brought the danger of crocodiles, so they always kept a watchful eye for these large animals.

SALTWATER PEOPLE

Aboriginal People who live on the coastal fringes of Australia are generally known as saltwater people and their hunting is ruled by the sea and the tides, but they also have an impressive knowledge of the ocean environment. Saltwater people have a deep spiritual and cultural connection to the sea and the ocean, and they believe that if they disrespect the ocean, it will not provide them with fish. Saltwater people hunt in mangrove swamps, estuaries, rivers, beaches and along reefs. Coastal saltwater people delight in collecting different varieties of shellfish including oysters off the rocks, mud mussels and mangrove snails from the mangroves and cockles from beneath the sand and rock pools. They thrive on the diverse and abundant source of marine life.

Coastal people have different hunting tools so that they can spear fish, stingrays, crabs and turtles. They only hunt for what they need, never more than they could eat. Most of the shellfish and fresh fish were caught and cooked before they were eaten, but there are a few animals that are eaten fresh like mangrove worms and oysters, and turtle eggs were drunk to quench their thirst while they were out hunting.

THE TROPICAL ZONES

To understand the diverse climate and weather patterns in Australia you firstly have to understand the breakdown of the three tropical climate zones in northern Australia. This will give you a better understanding of the two main seasons which the northern people know as the wet and dry seasons.

The zones are broken up into three parts:

Equatorial zone one

This area ranges from the tip of Cape York Peninsula to Bathurst, Melville Island and the north of Darwin in the Northern Territory zone.

Tropical zone two

This zone spreads right across the northern regions of Australia including Cape York (again), the top end of the Northern Territory, areas south of the Gulf of Carpentaria and the Kimberley region in Western Australia.

Subtropical zone three

This zone covers the coastal and inland fringe from Cairns, along the Queensland coast and hinterland, to the northern areas of New South Wales, and the coastal fringe north of Perth to Geraldton in Western Australia.

THE WET AND DRY SEASONS

Around the world everyone is familiar with the four seasons (summer, autumn, winter and spring) that change every three months. In the tropical zones of northern Australia there are only two key seasons. These seasons last for approximately six months each. The wet season, otherwise known as the Monsoon, starts its build-up of rain clouds around August but will commence its downpour of rain in November through to March. It is actually hotter than the dry season, with temperatures soaring between 30 and 50 degrees Celsius. This is caused by the high humidity and build-up of moisture in the air from the high volumes of water on the ground caused by extreme flooding.

The dry season on the other hand is what it states. Everything is so dry. This period also lasts for six months, commencing around April and lasting through to October. With clear blue skies, the temperature will reach around 20 degrees Celsius. But the land gets punished from the dry heat and the burning sun rays which dry up the land, grass and waterholes.

The build-up to the wet season lasts 3–4 months between the wet and dry. This is the humid time of the year, the time when everyone becomes edgy as they swelter in the humidity and wait for the first rains to fall. People in the Cape York region call it the Mango rain – the first rain that comes to give the mango trees a drink while they start to bear fruit. People in the Kimberley region call it the silly season as people tend to do silly things due to heat exhaustion and dealing with the prolonged humidity, which lasts all day and all night with no break. When the rains finally fall, they bring welcome relief to all the people, as well as the lands and animals as they cool everything down.

During extreme flooding in the wet season it's difficult to get around as the ground becomes soaked and boggy. This generally means hunting season is over for a few months. For this time of the year, Aboriginal People prepare themselves and stock up on food and water. But back in the days of our traditional ancestors, this time of the year meant they would head for the high lands, up to the hill tops where they could reside in a warm and dry cave for months on end, and from where they could have a full view of the vast lands below them. They would sometimes travel down the hill on foot when they needed to go off hunting for large animals to feed the tribe.

The tropical zone in the Northern Territory and Kimberley areas relies on a basic seasonal calendar. This helps the people to prepare for extreme weather such as cyclones, flooding, severe storms and bushfires which affect the road access in and out of the remote communities and towns. These extreme weathers also impact the livelihood of the community and map out the hunting and gathering seasons for what is in and out of season.

Month	European Season	Northern Tropical Seasons	Descriptions
January	Summer	Wet season	The wet season
February	Summer	Wet season	The wet season
March	Autumn	Wet season	The end of the rains
April	Autumn	Dry season	The end of the rains
May	Autumn	Dry season	The hot start of the dry
June	Winter	Dry season	The hot start of the dry
July	Winter	Dry season	The cooler dry
August	Winter	Build-up season	The cooler dry
September	Spring	Build-up season	The humid times begin
October	Spring	Build-up season	The humid times begin
November	Spring	Wet season	The first rains begin
December	Summer	Wet season	The first rains begin

Storytelling

I was situated in a campground called Punsand Bay in Far North Queensland, Cape York, at the tip of Australia. I had made my way up there to film 10 stories for a program on NITV called *Around the Campfire*. I was on a deadline and was putting extreme pressure on myself to rise to an expectation that I felt everyone had of me. As I chipped away at all my projects at once, 10 films and the final manuscript of *Bush Tukka Guide*, I felt a wave of excitement and fear rush over me. It was the final day on which I needed to send off my written content.

As I completed the last bit of writing whilst sitting on the beach, reality started to kick in. A voice in my head saying 'What do you think you're doing? You're not good enough.' I understood it was just my mind trying to jeopardise my work and self-confidence, so I had to find a way to overcome my fears and doubts. I told myself that this is the greatest opportunity I could ever have and it's for my people – it's preserving our cultural knowledge from an Aboriginal woman's perspective.

Fast forward exactly one year to the day. By some twist of fate, I am holidaying at the exact same campground in Punsand Bay – this was not planned.

I'm at my camp, cleaning my campervan, when a lady comes over and politely asks if I was Samantha Martin – the Bush Tukka Woman. She started to tell me a big story about how it's her husband's birthday today and he's an Indigenous man. She had just given him a copy of my book that morning for his present and was wondering if I would come say hi and wish him a happy birthday – how could I refuse that?

I went over and he looked up from the book; the expression on his face said he recognised who I was. He showed me the picture on the back and said 'Is this you sis?' I said, 'Yeah bro, that's me.' After a big round of hugs, I thanked them for their support and asked if they were interested in hearing a story about how the book came to be. I told them about my experience: the fear, and the mental and emotional journey I had gone through writing it. As I was signing his book I asked for the date and, in that instant, realised that it was this exact day one year earlier when I had sent the final manuscript to my publisher. We were all very ecstatic because this day now represented so much for all of us. For me it was confirmation that I had done exactly what I was meant to do when I wrote the book and all those doubts and fears I had felt a year ago were for nothing. It gave me a sense of pride and encouragement that if I could impress a cultural brother who hunted and lived off the land like this, I had done something right!

So, this experience revealed to me that we all have to believe in ourselves and be our own number one supporters. It helped me understand that our mob have been waiting for this kind of book for a long time. Throughout the years I have received hundreds of messages from people telling me how much they loved my book and how it had inspired them or connected them with their culture. My book has travelled the world and been used in schools and educational programs. It's been taken out on Country and held in the hands of young and old. I've seen copies so well used they're tattered and torn.

So on that note, I would like to thank everyone for supporting my humble little book!

Before you begin ...

Exploring the world of bush tukka is exciting and can unlock a new world of flavours, learnings and experiences. However, there are some things you must always be mindful of before you take to the land or seas:

- Respect our bush tukka and the lands, seas, skies, animals and plants, and the Traditional Owners of the places you visit along the way. Always respect the customs of the Traditional Owners of the land you're on, first and foremost.
- Our ancestors were always mindful to only take what they needed, and to never damage the plants they foraged from. We must all be committed to the same sustainable practices to protect our wildlife.
- Ensure you have correctly identified anything before you eat it – there are many plants and animals that are poisonous when consumed and can be easily misidentified. Purchasing your bush tukka (particularly from an Aboriginal and/or Torres Strait Islander–owned business) can be an ideal way to explore bush tukka if you're unfamiliar with it.
- Many of the plants and animals featured in this book are endangered and have only been included to preserve and share the knowledge passed down through the generations. Before harvesting or hunting, you should always consult with the relevant state and/or federal departments. There may be total bans or limits to how much you can take and what species you can hunt.

Plants

toxic properties

medicinal properties

recipe

FRUIT

Blue quandong

ABORIGINAL NAME/S

murrgan
Djabugay tribe, Kuranda, Far North Queensland

BOTANICAL NAME

Elaeocarpus angustifolius

Blue quandong trees are native to the rainforest areas of south-east Queensland and northern New South Wales. They grow well in the moist soil of subtropical rainforests, mostly around water systems such as rivers or creek lines, and are best known as the rainforest giants soaring as high as 40–50m into the sky. Aside from their height, they are easy to spot amongst the other rainforest trees because their long, glossy, dark-green leaves grow to an average length of 10–18cm. The leaves turn from green to a vibrant red colour just before they fall to the ground.

The flowers are clusters of bell-shaped, green–white petals, which start flowering in autumn–early summer and are a delicious treat for rainbow lorikeets.

The fruits are bright blue, growing up to 20mm in diameter with a thin layer of edible green flesh under the skin. Blue quandongs are not only popular bush foods amongst Aboriginal People, but also among the native wildlife, especially flying foxes, woompoo pigeons and cassowaries. Legends have been told by rainforest people in Far North Queensland that the cassowary got its blue colouring from eating too many blue quandongs. Having a bitter, floury taste, the blue fruit are best eaten fresh; once they dry out they don't offer a pleasant flavour for your palate.

TRADITIONAL USE

The blue quandong stone is hard, brown in colour and has grooves all around it, like a walnut. It was used by local Aboriginal women to make necklaces, and in recent times quandong necklaces have been coming back into fashion.

The fruit, although very dry in texture, keeps you hydrated for hours. Aboriginal women and children would scrape off the flesh by the river and make a paste out of it, which they ate when they needed to hydrate.

OTHER USES

People have been known to pickle and jam blue quandongs, which offer a bitter, tangy flavour. It is great to use in stews with red meats because they sustain the bitter flavour better.

Boab nut

ABORIGINAL NAME/S

Joongari

Wilinggin tribe, East Kimberley region, WA

BOTANICAL NAME

Adansonia gregorii

Boab trees are a Kimberley icon, growing right across from the west coast of the Kimberley to the east, into the Northern Territory. Every boab tree is unique; they grow tall, skinny, fat and round. They range from 10 to 15m in height and 9 to 12m in width. The leaves are a bright lime–dark green and shaped like a star.

The boab tree drops its leaves in the dry season, and then commences a new growth around September–early October, ready to flower in November. The flowers are spectacular to look at; light cream in colour, they start as pods, then the petals peel back revealing long brushes of pollen stems which produce a magnificent perfume. The flowers open early in the evening and are pollinated that night, lasting only one or two days on the tree before falling to the ground.

The boab tree produces boab nuts, which are hard pods with a light brown fur that grows on the outside. This fur should be scraped off because it can cause itchiness if direct contact is made with skin. The hard pod is broken open to reveal the fruit, a white, powdery pith that contains at least 10–20 seeds (bigger nuts contain even more seeds). The powdery pith inside the nut, along with the seeds, is what can be eaten. It has a sherbet texture and a sour, tangy flavour.

TRADITIONAL USE

The boab tree is also known as the bottle tree among Aboriginal People because of its unique, bottle-like shape. Aboriginal People throughout the Kimberley use every part of the boab tree: they use the bark to make strong, thick twine; the trunk to produce water by banging it until it softened, then stripping off the stringy fibres and wringing them out to release the water; the fruit for food and medicinal purposes to treat gastro and constipation. The shells of the pods are used as cups to collect water, and as bowls and utensils.

To create a sweet treat, Aboriginal women and children would collect ripe nuts and break them open to expose the soft yellowish pith and seeds inside. The pith and seeds were then crushed and mixed with water and sugarbag droplets, and then eaten; it is very tasty. Young or unripe fruit were buried in warm ground to make them ripe and ready to eat (this was the more traditional way of eating them). The seeds found inside the pith can also be dried and eaten like peanuts. The men preferred the boab nut young, while the inside is still soft and sticky. They would place the whole young nut on hot coals and let it roast through. It tastes very similar to roasted wild yams – sweet, warm and mushy.

To this day Aboriginal People still carve on the boab nuts using a pocketknife or a sharp tool. These carved nuts are famous among tourists who like to take a little bit of Kimberley treasure home with them.

OTHER USES

The fruit of the boab nut can taste sweet or sour, depending on how fresh it is; a fresh fruit has a sweet, tangy flavour. They have been used to make boab chocolates, muffins, bread and cakes. Dried boab flakes are sprinkled over salads to add a tangy flavour. You can make jams and chutneys using boab nuts.

People also sell boab roots commercially, promoting the benefits of its high fibre and high vitamin C content, as well as its richness in other minerals.

FLOWER

Bottlebrush

ABORIGINAL NAME/S

Birdak
Noongar tribe, WA

BOTANICAL NAME

Callistemon

Bottlebrushes are the little shrub with many names, but they are most commonly known simply as the bottlebrush. There are various species, which come in a range of colours, though the crimson bottlebrush is most popular in gardens across the country. Extensive studies have found there to be over 40 different species of *Callistemon* across the eastern and southern parts of Australia.

The natural habitats for bottlebrushes are in Australia's tropical north to the moderate southern lands. They can also be found growing in swamps or wet environment, such as along creek beds or in areas which are prone to floods.

The bottlebrush flowers are a spectacular flower that resembles a traditional bottle brush. As well as red, bottlebrush flowers come in cream, yellow and pink blooms, the brush being made up of a number of individual flowers called filaments. They flower in late winter and spring. The flowers produce nectars that are absolutely irresistible to the birds and insects.

The seeds of the bottlebrush are tiny, hard bubble-like seeds that sit on the flower stem in a little cluster. They will not be released for a few years, but in some species the fruits can be encouraged to blossom with the help of bushfires. The leaves of many bottlebrushes are very ornamental and, in some species, are covered with fine, soft hairs. You'll also find them to be very hardy and spiky and can prick when pressed too hard, though they will release a lemony scent when bruised.

TRADITIONAL USE

The flowers have always been eaten by Aboriginal People and are sweet from the nectar. You can bang the flowers on your hand to release the nectar and lick it off your hand. It was, and still is, very popular amongst children and women.

OTHER USES

You can boil the flowers in hot water to create a sweet tea – as the water turns brown, it's time to drink. The sweet lemon-scented tea makes for a refreshing drink, offering natural sweetening that is full of antiviral and antifungal properties.

NUT

Bunya nut

ABORIGINAL NAME/S

bunyi bunyi
Kabi Kabi tribe, Sunshine Coast, Queensland

BOTANICAL NAME

Araucaria bidwillii

Bunya pine trees grow from Far North and south-east Queensland to northern New South Wales; in subtropical rainforests and in the hinterland among moist soil, mostly on mountain-tops. They grow as tall as 30–45m, with rough-barked trunks to protect them from the cold winds, and sharp-pointed, dark-green leaves about 2.5cm long. The bunya pines also produce large green cones about the same size as a football but weighing approximately 10kg.

The cones can be found during late January–early March. The female cone produces 50–100 bunya nuts, which grow inside beige shells, held together around the stem of the cone by a waxy, white sap. To remove the kernels from the cone, simply pull them off from the base of the cone with your hands.

The shells are soft (but tough) fibrous packages which need to be peeled back to get to the actual bunya nuts. Each shell contains one teardrop-shaped bunya nut, approximately 6cm long. The easiest way to get to the nut is to boil the shells for up to 30 minutes, until the water turns slightly brown, or you can see each shell develop a small split at the tip. You can then peel the shells open with a knife.

TRADITIONAL USE

The Kabi Kabi word for bunya pine was *bon-yi*, which, over time, turned into *bun-ya*. Bunya nuts were a staple food of the Aboriginal People living in south-east Queensland. They ate them raw or roasted them on hot coals. Every year in bunya season, bunya nuts were collected from all over the region to hold a bunya gathering and feasting. Many tribes would put aside their differences and gather in the mountains for their yearly bunya nut feast.

Traditionally, young Aboriginal warriors would climb the rough-barked trees to get the young cones and then carry them all the way back down to the ground. The climb is extremely challenging because the tree trunk has hard, rough, very sharp bark that can slice your foot if you don't know the correct climbing techniques. The climb was done in ceremony and was taken extremely seriously; only the fittest of the warriors were chosen to climb the tree.

OTHER USES

Bunya nuts are a great bush food and very versatile. When eaten raw they taste slightly sweet and are crunchy in texture; it is similar to eating a raw sweet potato. To cook the nuts, it's as simple as boiling or roasting them whole, or cooking them on the barbecue.

Once they are cooked the bunya nut looks like a giant pine nut, but it is easier to open and tastes very similar to a chestnut, sweet with a floury, waxy texture.

People have found many ways to introduce bunya nuts into their cooking. The nuts can be used in making soups, using the nuts to replace potatoes. They can also be pickled or made into pesto, or used in beef casseroles, damper, scones, cakes and desserts such as biscuits.

Burdekin plum

ABORIGINAL NAME/S

guybalam
Djabugay tribe, Kuranda, Far North Queensland

BOTANICAL NAME

Pleiogynium timorense

Burdekin plum trees can grow as large as 20–30m in height and are predominantly found along coastal areas, creek banks and in rainforest areas in tropical Far North Queensland. They belong to the mango family.

Burdekin plum trees are distinctive looking, with a strong trunk (which is grey in patches) and dark, rough bark. They have long, rubbery-looking branches on which the plums grow in bunches of 2–10, sometimes more. The leaves range in colour from dark to light green, and grow to about 10cm in length and 4–6cm in width. Eight to 10 leaves grow on a single stalk, and the flowers are small, creamy-white constellations.

The plums are deep purple, almost black, and they grow to the size of a 50-cent piece, but can vary in size depending on the environment. The fruit grows in winter months. They have a thin layer of purple flesh which surrounds a large, hard, woody seed, and are quite tarty in flavour; the riper the fruit, the sweeter the flavour. But they do not ripen on the trees. Instead, they ripen from the ground-surface temperature when they fall.

TRADITIONAL USE

Burdekin plums were, and still are, very popular with local Aboriginal People. They enjoy eating the tarty, tangy plums fresh or cooked. Traditionally, the women and children would crush the plums into a paste; because the fruit is made up of approximately 70 per cent water, it offered a great way to hydrate on long, hot days.

OTHER USES

Burdekin plums are highly sought after by people in Far North Queensland who enjoy making jams, jellies, cakes and cookies from the fruit. They make great chutney, and savoury or sweet sauces which go well with pork, chicken, lamb and beef.

Burdekin plums contain vitamin C and are high in fibre and other natural minerals.

VEGETABLE

Bush onion

ABORIGINAL NAME/S

jurnda
Jaru tribe, Western Desert, East Kimberley, WA

BOTANICAL NAME

Cyperus bulbosus

Bush onion plants look like grass clusters, and grow in the Kimberley region of Western Australia and in central Australia. They are found in the coastal dunes and sand hills of the floodplains as well as on the fringes of saltmarsh flats.

Above the ground, the bush onion grows as a thin, spindly, vibrant green blade of grass that turns yellow when dry.

It is best to gather the onions when the grass is yellow and dry. The small edible bulbs grow around the roots, so to find the bush onions you have to first identify the right grass blades, whether green or yellow in colour, then break the surface with a digging stick to loosen the sand. Once the sand is loose, gently spread the sand away with your fingers creating a raking effect. With the spreading of the sand, the small, brown bulbs will appear in clusters growing around the roots. Inside they are cream in colour and rubbery in texture. Though bland in flavour, they are filling: it doesn't take long before you gather enough to feed a family.

The onions can be eaten raw, or cooked in hot ashes. The tiny bulb also has a thin but tough brown husk around it that can be easier to remove after cooking in hot ashes.

The bulbs become translucent after cooking them on the coals. They are very much like brown onions in shape and colour but taste totally different, more like pine nuts or chestnuts.

TRADITIONAL USE

Bush onions are an important bush food for Kimberley Aboriginal People, and the best time to look for jurnda is after the wet season, around April–May.

When gathering bush onions Aboriginal People light a fire and then go off gathering so that the fire burns down to lovely hot ashes, ready for when they return with their buckets and buckets of onions.

There is a process for how to husk the onions to save time and energy, as it can be a tedious process if not done properly. Once the fire has died down, the Kimberley Aboriginal People remove the hot ash from the top and place handfuls of onions in the remaining hot ash, covering them with the ash previously removed. They leave them for about 5 minutes and then with a stick they unearth the onions, moving the ash to one side. They proceed to collect as many onions as their hands can hold, they then rub their hands together to create friction, rubbing the onions against one another until the husks start to peel away. Then they throw the onions in the air to let the husks blow away and catch the onions in their hands. They repeat this about 3–4 times; it's the only effective way to husk the pea-sized onions.

OTHER USES

Jurnda can also be crushed up and turned into a paste, flattened out to be made into a flat bread and then thrown back onto the coals to cook for about 10 minutes.

Bush passionfruit

ABORIGINAL NAME/S

yidiringgi
Jaru tribe, Western Desert, East Kimberley, WA

BOTANICAL NAME

Passiflora foetida

Bush passionfruit is a weed-like vine that grows all over other trees and shrubs. This particular plant is actually an introduced species, but I've included it as it's become a favourite for many Aboriginal People. This climbing vine is commonly found in the northern parts of Australia, from the borders of Byron Bay in New South Wales, across to Port Hedland in Western Australia. The vine thrives on warm, humid–dry tropical weather around rocky hills, swamps, creeks, riverbeds and coastal areas – wherever there is a water system. The vine and leaves are waxy in texture.

Each leaf has three points, similar to the common passionfruit leaf. This distinctive vine can be recognised by the delicate furry casing resembling a net, wherein the passionfruit grows to the size of a grape. The casing starts off lime green in colour and then changes to bright orange or yellow. **Do not eat the fruit when they are green as they are highly toxic at this stage.** Inside the bright orange or yellow casing there is a soft, grey, juicy flesh with about 5–7 black seeds. Aboriginal People ate everything, the skin and seeds, but because the shell is very thin, the seeds can also be sucked out. The wild fruits are best during mid-summer, around December–February.

The flower on the bush passionfruit is one of the most stunning flowers you will ever see. It looks like a delicate orchid. Each flower is a wonderful mixture of white, light and dark purples, and light and dark greens.

TRADITIONAL USE

Wild passionfruit are a favourite treat amongst Aboriginal People. They are eaten fresh from the vines and can be a refreshing treat on hot days.

OTHER USES

Wild bush passionfruit are everywhere and are easily accessible to anyone who would like to introduce these sweet golden treats into their kitchen. They work well raw, on cheese platters or in fruit salads; just wash them and drop them in whole or squeeze the seeds over the fruit salad.

If you dry the flowers out, they make a great sleep-time tea.

Bush passionfruit is full of vitamin C and antioxidants, providing a natural source of vitamins and minerals to maintain a healthy immune system.

Bush sugarbag

ABORIGINAL NAME/S

ngarlu

Jaru tribe, Western Desert, East Kimberley, WA

guku
Yolŋu tribe, Arnhem Land, NT

SCIENTIFIC NAME

Austroplebeia australis (previously called *Trigona australis*)

There are over 1500 species of native bees in Australia and only 10 of those species are non-stinging bees, also known as social native bees. These bees produce bush sugarbag.

Social native bees are about half a centimetre long, and blue-black in colour, with hairy, extended back legs, which carry the nectar and pollen. They are known to be found in warmer, tropical areas such as the northern half of Western Australia, the Northern Territory, Queensland and the northern and coastal areas of New South Wales.

Social native bees are attracted to native plants, and can live in artificial nests with good, warm insulation; hollow logs make the best nests. Different non-stinging bees make different types of entrances to their hives depending on their environment; some entrances are narrow, others are wide. When you spot a honey nest, tap on the trunk to find the hollow point before you chop the whole tree down, look for a small brown waxy 'nose' or mound – the bees' entrance into the tree. When you have located the entrance, take an axe and slice the branch to reveal the opening; you will see the yellow larvae and then the honey pods.

Bush sugarbag is dark brown in colour and can be found in tree hollows where social native bees have made their nests. These bees are not aggressive, but, if you disturb their nests, they will swarm around you and stick to your skin or hair.

Social native bees produce and store small amounts of bush sugarbag with dark brown wax. The bush sugarbag is tangy in flavour but has a delicious bush-flower aroma. The honey pods are round and very different to the commercial bee pods; they look like a bunch of round, golden-brown grapes stacked neatly next to each other.

NOTE: Due to the decline of native bees, we do not encourage the harvesting of bush sugarbag.

TRADITIONAL USE

Aboriginal People are able to spot a beehive high up in a tree; it can be as simple as seeing a small, waxy hole at the end of a branch or spotting the small black bees, which look very similar to flies, flying in and out of the hole. I have known my aunties to follow a single bee to its hive, which is a difficult thing to do out in the middle of the bush, but they found the hive and were rewarded with the most delicious, sweet, silky-smooth honey.

Aboriginal People use the honey as a little sweet treat, but they also use it to treat sore throats by eating it, and infected wounds or skin rashes by smearing it over the infected areas.

Sugarbag is highly prized, especially by the men. They would harvest the dark brown wax to use when making their tools and weapons such as axes, spears and woomeras (a traditional spear throwing device). They would prepare the wax by chewing and squeezing it to remove the honey. Then they would use the wax to attach the axe heads to the handles by heating it and moulding it over the wooden handles. They would place the axe head on top and then, using natural twine, bind the wax and the axe head in place.

The wax was, and still is, used for the mouthpieces on didgeridoos, or yidakis.

OTHER USES

Bush sugarbag can get very messy when being collected in the wild, but if you can strain the honey and collect enough of it, it is good to use in the same way as common honey: as a spread on bread, or to add to your cooking, salads, cereals or in teas. Bush sugarbag can also be used in a medicinal way as it contains antibacterial properties. A teaspoon of sugarbag honey can treat sore throats, chest infections, colds or flus.

FRUIT

Bush tomato

ABORIGINAL NAME/S

eerlud
Wilinggin tribe, East Kimberley, WA

BOTANICAL NAME

Solanum centrale

The bush tomato is a small desert plant, approximately 30cm in height, with grey to bronze leaves and attractive mauve–blue flowers. It grows well in the hot, dry climates throughout the central deserts: from Tennant Creek in the Northern Territory to Marla in South Australia and the East Kimberley in Western Australia.

In the red sandy desert, these plants grow quickly after summer rains, mainly from dormant rootstock which can last for many years between favourable seasons. The plants also respond and grow rapidly after soil disturbance (along roadsides) or after bushfires. In the wild they fruit for only two months.

There are 100 species of wild tomatoes in Australia, however only six are known to be edible. **The other *Solanum* are highly toxic. They contain high levels of solanine which is known to be poisonous.** If you are not familiar with this plant, do not experiment with it as the poison can cause severe stomach aches, vomiting, diarrhoea, and it can be fatal.

These desert tomatoes are known for their sweet and slightly tangy flavour. They are the most well known and certainly the most consumed species of bush tomatoes. Eerlud grow between 1 and 3cm in diameter, and are yellow when ripened.

These days, bush tomatoes are grown commercially by Aboriginal communities in the deserts of central Australia. Using irrigation, they have extended the fruiting season to eight months, offering a longer supply of bush tomatoes to the commercial culinary industry.

TRADITIONAL USE

Eerlud is an important bush food. This arid-lands fruit has been a staple food of the Aboriginal desert-dwellers of central Australia for many thousands of years. The traditional harvesting method is to collect the sun-dried fruits off the small bush in the autumn and winter months. In its dried form, bush tomato can be stored for several years.

Traditionally eerlud offered a treat for the women and children, who ate the fruit fresh. The fruits are believed to build immunity, while also nourishing and hydrating the body from the heat. But if too many are eaten, it can act as a laxative.

FRUIT

Aboriginal People also use the roots of this plant to treat toothache. The roots can be baked in ash and then peeled, crushed and placed on the aching tooth.

OTHER USES

Bush tomato has a strong sun-dried tomato flavour and aroma when dried. It is just delicious in recipes with white or game meats such as fish, chicken or pork. It also offers a lovely Aboriginal twist to homemade dukkah or pasta sauce, and adds a great smoky flavour to marinades for pork, beef ribs, steaks or roasts.

The dried fruit is normally ground and used as a seasoning, rather than used whole. It is particularly suitable for use in casseroles and soups, giving a rich, robust flavour. This bush food has a variety of uses but should be used fairly sparingly. Its strong flavour can quickly overpower more delicate food, especially if used in quiches, or with eggs or cheeses. The bush tomato compliments the traditional ingredients used in Mediterranean-style cooking such as eggplant, olives or capsicum. Ground bush tomato is best kept cool and dry, and has a considerable shelf life.

FRUIT

Cluster fig

ABORIGINAL NAME/S

ngalga-yarrubadjal
Djabugay tribe, Kuranda, Far North Queensland

BOTANICAL NAME

Ficus racemosa

Cluster fig trees are magnificent, reaching up to 30–35m high, with large, green leaves. They are known as majestic giants, and grow along riverbanks, riverine forest and in much drier environments that have underground water systems. They grow mostly in Western Australia, Northern Territory, north-east Queensland and south-east Queensland.

Playing an important part in the ecosystem, cluster fig trees provide food for humans and animals, natural medicines and shade along the waterways.

Cluster fig trees are easy to recognise because the figs grow on the branches and trunks in clusters. The clusters change colour at different times, from light green to yellow, orange and then to red when the fruits have ripened. The figs are produced around September–December. The figs that grow on the external root system of the tree are much sweeter in flavour and, like common figs, have hundreds of little seeds inside. But the cluster figs are often infested with insects and larvae, so best check before taking a bite.

TRADITIONAL USE

This remarkable species of tree offered several different methods for survival to the Aboriginal People who relied on cluster figs not only as a main food source, but also used other parts of the tree for medicinal purposes and to make tools and canoes.

They would scrape off the inner bark and boil it in water to produce a liquid that was good for treating diarrhoea. They would also hollow out the soft, inner part of the trunk to make canoes and coolamons because the wood is light, strong and waterproof.

OTHER USES

The cluster fig tree will provide great shade in your garden and will attract an array of wildlife from birds to insects, but ensure you do not plant a cluster fig tree near buildings, paving, sewer lines or houses, as their aggressive root system does grow extremely fast and will damage whatever is in its way.

Cluster figs work well in jams and chutneys. You can also bake them, then drizzle them with a syrupy sauce and add ice-cream on the side for a delicious dessert.

Conkerberry

ABORIGINAL NAME/S

Unknown

BOTANICAL NAME

Carissa lanceolata

Conkerberries, also known as bush currants, are native mainly to the Top End and central Australia, but are also found in the Kimberley in Western Australia, and around Cape York in Far North Queensland. They grow in a wide range of terrains and soil types in hot, dry climates.

The plant is a multi-stemmed shrub, 1–3m high and 1.5–4m wide. Its leaves are glossy green, narrow and 1–5cm long. It has hard thorns, also 1–5cm long. The white, star-shaped flowers, about 1cm wide, have a sweet scent and grow in December–January. The small berries, 1–2cm long, appear in

February–March. They turn dark purple, or even black, when ripe and have a sweet taste.

This plant also becomes a weed in Australian grazing lands. It can multiply fast by natural layering. In such cases, it becomes a menace and is difficult to control, even with herbicides.

TRADITIONAL USE

Aboriginal People frequently eat conkerberries, as their sweet taste is refreshing.

The conkerberry tree was also traditionally used in other ways by Aboriginal People. They burnt the wood of the tree and used the smoke created to treat colds and coughs by inhaling. The leaves were boiled and the liquid swallowed, also to treat colds. The orange roots were cut, chipped and burnt, and the smoke was used to keep bad spirits away from children up to their early teenage years. This smoke also chases away mosquitoes, and was placed on a fire when mosquitoes were in the area. The branches of the conkerberry tree were often used as a bush broom to sweep up around camp. And the V-shaped part of the branches was used to form the hook part of a woomera (a traditional spear throwing device).

OTHER USES

Conkerberries are still a secret. They can be used to make desserts such as conkerberry cheesecakes and conkerberry scones, and can also be added to fruit salads.

Davidson's plum

ABORIGINAL NAME/S

ooray
Jirrbal (Dyirbal) tribe, Far North Queensland

munumba
Djabugay tribe, Kuranda, Far North Queensland

jirirr
Kuku Yalanji tribe, Far North Queensland

BOTANICAL NAME

Davidsonia pruriens

The famous Davidson's plum is a popular rainforest plum that grows best in warmer subtropical and tropical environments. Davidson's plums, as they're commonly known, grow on tall slender trees with no branches. Most trees will grow to about 10m high, but can reach up to 20m in height in its natural rainforest environment of north-east Queensland and New South Wales. The leaves are unique: large feather-like glossy green leaves with thick rib veins and spiky edges.

The trees will flower from November to February, with clusters of red and yellow flower blossoms growing on stems off the trunk. Dangling from under the canopy of the large droopy umbrella leaves, the fruits will start to develop from February to May and continue to grow and ripen through to August–September. They are the most incredible fruit, starting off a pale green colour, which later turns into a deep black–purple colour with a waxy coating on the outer layer. The inside of the fruit is a vibrant red flesh with no seeds.

Although they look plump and sweet, the fruits are quite deceiving as they are very sour and tart. When the fruits ripen, they will naturally fall to the ground.

TRADITIONAL USE

For thousands of years, Aboriginal People have eaten the fruits fresh from the trees for hydration. They had the knowledge that the fruits contained a lot of healthy vitamins which helped sores and inflammation and any other viral infection. They used the plums for burns and stings as they are a great cooling agent.

OTHER USES

The most common use for ooray are in jams, relishes, chutneys, syrups and even wines. Because the fruit is so bitter and sour, it needs a lot of sugar to balance the bitterness. They offer a lot of health benefits of a super fruit, full of antioxidants, vitamin C, potassium, lutein, vitamin E, folate, zinc, magnesium and calcium.

FRUIT

Desert lime

ABORIGINAL NAME/S

Unknown

BOTANICAL NAME

Citrus glauca

Australian desert limes are from a tree species belonging to the citrus family. These trees grow inland, in dry areas like western Queensland, particularly around the Roma district in the south-west. They also grow in New South Wales and South Australia. They are the quickest citrus tree species in the world to set fruit after flowering. They have also evolved to protect themselves against grazing animals by growing sharp thorns. However, the trees cease to have any thorns on growth above the browsing height of large kangaroos!

Desert lime trees are slow growing, like most of the Australian native citrus species. The small, multi-stemmed, dense trees grow up to 12m high, and have slender, upward-facing leaves, 5–8mm wide. Small, white flowers are produced around August and the fruit ripens by November–December. The fruits look like tiny, grape-sized lemons with a porous rind and juicy, but sour, centre.

NOTE: Over-harvesting and incorrect harvesting methods have had a significant impact on wild desert lime trees. Please limit how much you take, or purchase commercially where possible.

TRADITIONAL USE

Desert limes are eaten raw by Aboriginal People to quench their thirst.

OTHER USES

Desert limes have three times the amount of vitamin C found in oranges. They require no peeling, de-seeding or other preparation, and can be used in any product or process where 'normal' limes or lemons are used; the main differences being their small size, lack of peel and more intense flavour. They can be frozen without losing flavour or presentation characteristics when thawed for later use.

One of the best ways to use desert limes is when cooking fish in foil or paperbark; drizzle the juice over the fish. Desert limes can also be used in sauces, marmalades, pickles and chutneys. One of my favourite uses is in desert lime sorbet. You can also try them in a cocktail or punch, for a great look and wonderful lime twist.

The versatility of this fruit, its tarty, tangy flavours and its outback origins allow it to be admired by food enthusiasts.

Green plum

ABORIGINAL NAME/S

garlay
Wilinggin tribe, East Kimberley, WA

BOTANICAL NAME

Buchanania obovata

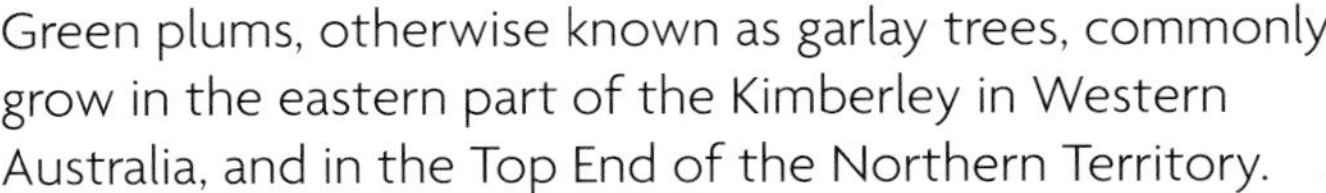

Green plums, otherwise known as garlay trees, commonly grow in the eastern part of the Kimberley in Western Australia, and in the Top End of the Northern Territory.

Growing as tall as 5–10m, with round-edged, light-green leaves that are about 12cm long, these trees are found in rugged terrains close to creeks and rivers. The Kimberley region has two seasons, a dry season and a wet season. The dry season lasts from May–October, and the wet season lasts from November–April. Garlay trees start to flower in September (the middle of the wet season) with delicate, creamy-white

FRUIT

flowers, and they fruit from October to April (from the end of the wet season until the end of the dry season).

The garlay plum is a round, light-green plum, the size of a five-cent piece. The fruit has a hard, black seed inside and juicy, green flesh on the outside.

TRADITIONAL USE

Aboriginal People in the Kimberley consider the garlay a treasure. The women, men and children will spend hours collecting the fruit, filling buckets and buckets. Some people crush the flesh of the plums and create a paste to eat without the hard, black seeds getting in the way. Others just prefer to eat them whole.

OTHER USES

Garlay are used as a laxative to treat constipation. Rich in vitamin C and fibre, this little fruit offers a natural, healthy way to boost your immune system. The seeds can also be crushed up to get the nut inside which tastes very similar to a macadamia nut.

This green plum also offers a delicious sweet and tangy treat on a hot day.

FLOWER

Grevillea

ABORIGINAL NAME/S

Unknown

BOTANICAL NAME

Grevillea

Grevillea's are another beautiful native found in bushland and gardens all around Australia, easily identifiable by their unique flowers. The grevillea flowers have no petals, instead having a beautiful coil-like display with long, needle-like stems curling over and back into its pod like a loop.

The grevillea shrubs grow well in sunny, well-drained soil. They thrive in most climates, however, cold and frost tolerance varies between species. Its natural habitat is coastal environments. Grevilleas are also known to be very hardy and resilient plants and requires little to no maintenance. They are highly recommended in nurseries across Australia for hedging or screening, but also to enhance the visual appeal of any type of garden. The beauty of these native shrubs is the flowers, which come in many colours, from red and pink to yellow and gold. They're a great attraction to the native birds and bees due to the nectar.

Grevilleas also come in a great range of sizes, from groundcovers and mid-sized shrubs to tall screening plants, which are perfect for privacy.

Let's get back to the spectacular flower clusters: as highlighted earlier, the flowers have no petals and generally take one of three forms, toothbrush (stamens and styles emerge on one side of the stem, forming a toothbrush-looking effect), the spider (stamens and styles look like spindly spider legs) or the woolly bush (a more even arrangement of stamens like a brush). All types can flower throughout the year, including winter.

TRADITIONAL USE

This shrub is used as a mosquito repellent – the dry leaves are gathered up and burnt and the smoke will ward off the mosquitos. The flowers are also considered a sweet treat – Aboriginal People gather the flowers up and put them into a drum of water or coolamon (wooden carrying dish) to soak until all the nectars dilute into the water – the result is a drink similar to a cordial, offering a sweet drink on a hot day.

FRUIT

Kakadu plum

ABORIGINAL NAME/S

gubinge or kabiny plums
Bardi tribe, West Kimberley, WA

mudoorr
Jawi tribe, West Kimberley, WA

BOTANICAL NAME

Terminalia ferndinandiana

Kakadu plum (also known as gubinge, kabiny, billygoat plum or murunga) is a tree native to the tropical woodlands from north-western to eastern Arnhem Land, in the Northern Territory. It also grows in the east and west Kimberley regions, in Western Australia. A mature Kakadu plum tree grows to 15m high, with creamy-grey bark and large, oval-shaped leaves. Up to 10–20 plums grow on one long stem. The plums are sometimes light yellow but mostly light green.

They are an interesting shape, similar to an almond, about 2cm long and 1cm wide, with a very pointy end.

The Kakadu plum tree flowers between September–December, with small, creamy-white flowers growing along the stems and producing a sweet aroma. The tree fruits from March–June.

TRADITIONAL USE

The Bardi People (from the Dampier Peninsula, near Broome in Western Australia) use every part of the mudoorr tree, learning from their ancestors not to waste anything. From December–May, just after the wet season, the local Aboriginal People are still harvesting the fruit to meet demands. They not only eat the fruit from the tree, but they also eat the tree's sap by cooking it in a bowl over hot coals until it hardens. The bark is also used as bush medicine by boiling it and applying the liquid to the skin to heal rashes, infected sores and sunburn. This liquid is also drunk as a tea to treat inflammation in the joints.

OTHER USES

Kakadu plums have a sweet-and-sour flavour, very similar to dried apricots. They can be eaten raw or used raw in fruit salad.

Kakadu plums have become extremely popular within large health-food companies as a valued ingredient because they contain antibacterial, antiviral and antifungal properties, and much more. Kakadu plums reportedly have the highest concentration of vitamin C of any fruit tested in the world. For example, an orange contains 53mg of vitamin C and a Kakadu plum contains an average of 2907mg of vitamin C. Health-food companies are using Kakadu plums or gubinge to develop an organic vitamin C powder, and are also looking to use it in the cosmetic industry.

FRUIT

Lemon aspen

ABORIGINAL NAME/S

Unknown

BOTANICAL NAME

Acronychia acidula

Lemon aspen seems well adapted to tropical–subtropical rainforest, particularly in highland areas and will tolerate both full sun and semi-shade, although it prefers well-drained and fertile clay loam soils, with a sunny aspect and extra moisture when young. Lemon aspen can be found in north-eastern Queensland, occurring naturally from Cooktown to Mackay, but it can be grown much further south.

This tree grows up to 2m high and has dark green, elliptical leaves. Flowering in summer–late autumn, the delicate, white flowers have been observed to last only a few weeks, but they give off a stunningly sweet scent.

The small, cherry-sized fruit is about 1.5–2.5cm in diameter. It is a pale-lemon colour, and has a tough, star-shaped core – textured much like an apple core, and, similarly like an apple, with very small black seeds. The thin layer of flesh is slightly spongy. The fruit exudes an incredible tropical-citrus aroma (much more so when fresh) and has a sharp citrus flavour with lemon characteristics. Lemon aspen needs to be picked slightly under-ripe.

TRADITIONAL USE

Aboriginal People eat lemon aspen straight off the tree, enjoying its citrus flavours. They also will squash handfuls of the fruit into a container to extract the juice, which they drink to boost the immune system and to clear sore throats. The juice is also used as an antiseptic by rubbing it on sores or boils.

OTHER USES

The flavour of lemon aspen is extremely strong – 100g of lemon aspen equals something close to the juice, zest and pulp of about six large lemons. It works best in dressings, marinades and dishes where a little can be added at the last minute for a burst of freshness. This versatile fruit can be used in 100 different ways such as making jams, jellies and juice. Whole lemon aspen fruits or just the juice can be used in pastries, desserts and sauces. The pulp from juicing can also flavour shortbread, lemon aspen mayonnaise or lemon aspen vinegar. It is suggested that the leaves can also be used for flavouring. They are excellent in curds and salad dressings.

HERB

Lemon myrtle

ABORIGINAL NAME/S

djulungunu
Djabugay tribe, Kuranda, Far North Queensland

BOTANICAL NAME

Backhousia citriodora

A healthy lemon myrtle shrub grows to about 1–5m in height and 1.5m in width. It grows naturally in the cool, wet climate around northern and southern Queensland, and northern New South Wales, where it has been cultivated for commercial and private use. Sadly, the plant does not grow wildly anymore.

The shrub has an attractive, healthy look with full, lush branches that hang gracefully, holding long thin leaves which grow heavily on each branch, creating that full, bursting appeal. In autumn the shrub will grow stunning clusters of creamy-white flowers, which give off an intensely sweet, lemon fragrance. The shrub itself does not bear fruit. The leaves are the hero of this plant and are becoming a feature of Australian cuisine.

TRADITIONAL USE

Aboriginal People use this plant to keep hydrated by sucking on the leaves. This provides them with nutrients, vitamins and minerals, which fought off diseases and gave energy to the body. They also make use of the high antibacterial properties in the leaves by chewing them or crushing them into a paste to rub on sores or boils. The leaves can also be used as an insect repellent by burning them to create a thick smoke which keeps the mosquitos away.

OTHER USES

In cooking, lemon myrtle leaves can be used in a similar way to bay leaves in marinades, soups, stews, casseroles and roasts. The flavour can be intense and overpowering, but used properly it will complement chicken, beef, lamb and kangaroo dishes. For desserts, try using the dry, crushed leaves in cheesecake fillings or bases, apple crumble toppings, biscuits or cakes.

The plant also contains anti-inflammatory properties which can be used to treat swollen fingers, toes and joints by sucking on the leaves to release their natural oils, or by making a tea from them. To drink lemon myrtle as a tea, pluck a handful of leaves and add to a pot of boiling water; wait until the water and the leaves turn slightly brown. The tea can be drunk warm or cold, and you may like to add a teaspoon of honey for extra flavour or sweetness.

NUT

Macadamia

ABORIGINAL NAME/S

Unknown

BOTANICAL NAME

Macadamia integrifolia and
Macadamia tetraphylla

This mysterious tree belongs to the genus *Macadamia*, which encompasses four species of tree or shrub grown for their edible seeds or nuts. Macadamias can reach a height of 18-20m high and 15m wide and have a commercial lifespan of 40–60 years.

The leaves on the macadamia are dark green, glossy and leathery in texture. They are long, oval-shaped and have slight waves throughout, depending on the variety.

Growing 20-30cm long, they do not have veins but a spine running through the centre.

In spring the tree produces cream, white and pinkish flowers, which grow in tight clusters that dangle from the branches. Each flower has five petals and a stem growing out the centre. It looks very similar to the freshwater mangrove flowers. After flowering it produces the most incredible green, thick, leathery husks that are formed in bunches of up to 20 fruits. After the ripening process, the fruits will start to split around February to April, depending on the tree and its environment, to reveal the nuts. These nuts are round and up to 27mm in diameter; when the colour is glossy brown, they are ready to be eaten. What I enjoy about the macadamia is that you have to work hard to extract the delicious creamy nut inside. You need to peel the husk to get to the brown nut. Once you crack open the hard-cased nut, you will find the flesh that sits perfectly protected inside its ingenious casing. The nuts will fall to the ground when they are ripe.

TRADITIONAL USE

Traditionally, Aboriginal People harvested large amounts of macadamia nuts, as they were a high source of energy and protein and could fill them up for long periods of time. The hard layer of the shell is used for jewellery and its hard and sharp edges as a cutting tool.

OTHER USES

The uses of macadamia nuts are endless – they are a highly priced nut and are commonly found in supermarkets everywhere. They are mostly used in sweet dishes such as ice-creams, biscuits and cakes, but the nuts have many health benefits that make them a great addition to a range of cooking.

They are rich in monosaturated fats and are a high source of vitamins and minerals. Macadamia nuts have been well studied and there's evidence that consuming the nuts can help with many health problems, when eaten in their natural form with no added flavouring. They are proven to help reduce inflammation relating to heart disease, improve cellular and artery damage and reduce the risk of type 2 diabetes.

Midyim berry

ABORIGINAL NAME/S

Unknown

BOTANICAL NAME

Austromyrtus dulcis

Midyim berry, or sand berry as it's sometimes known, is a hardy bush food plant to grow. Midyim are small shrubs and can be found in sandy coastal areas, woodlands, and sub-rainforest fringes. This unique-looking berry is an absolute favourite for many Aboriginal People as it offers a sweet taste, with a slight hint of eucalyptus flavour. The midyim berries are closely related to lilly pillies. Midyim mostly grow on the east coast of Australia, northern to southern parts of Queensland and as far south as central New South Wales.

The leaves are 2–4cm long and 1–3mm wide. They are long needle-like and spindly-shaped, with a vibrant green colour. When young, the leaves are a slight maroon colour, then turn dark green with age- the leaves almost remind me of rosemary yet a lot more spread out.

Midyim flowers are white and delicate-looking with five oval-shaped petals that grow up to 7–10mm wide. They are usually grouped in tight clusters, on short stalks and in amongst the leafy foliage. In its natural habitat, flowers appear in spring, from September to November, and it will start to fruit in summer, from December to February.

The fruit is a berry: round, light-purple and dotted with dark-purple spots. The berries hold up to ten pale brown seeds. The berries are white all over and sprinkled with tiny light purple to brown spots which give them a greyish appearance. Some of the Kabi Kabi Elders have described these little berries as their sweet treats and people have made jams and pies using the berries. But for me personally, I do not know how they get them back to their kitchens; my trouble is, they are too scrumptious not to eat while harvesting them!

When harvesting the scrumptious sweet berries, it is wise to try to collect some to take home to experiment with them, making jams or adding them to smoothies or even muffins as a replacement for blueberries.

TRADITIONAL USE

Midyim berries were, and still are, a treat for Aboriginal People. The sweet, cinnamon-flavoured berries offer a high amount of vitamin C, antioxidants and fibre. The berries were mainly eaten by the women and children.

SPICE

Mountain bush pepper

ABORIGINAL NAME/S

Unknown

BOTANICAL NAME

Tasmannia lanceolata

Mountain bush pepper is a versatile little bush treasure. This small tree grows 2–5m high and 1–2m wide, with attractive, bright-red stems and glossy, dark-green leaves. It grows naturally in rainforest areas, in the cool, wet climate around southern New South Wales, and throughout Victoria and Tasmania.

It produces cream-coloured flowers from October to January, depending on its location. The berry-like fruits are 5–10mm in diameter, beginning dark red and turning shiny black when ripe in summer or autumn. The berries generally appear only on female trees, though plants of both sexes contain flowers. Plant growth is moderate to fast under the favourable conditions of a cool, wet climate.

TRADITIONAL USE

Traditionally mountain bush pepper was used to treat infections by eating it. Sore gums and toothaches are treated by crushing the pepper berries into a paste with a bit of water and applying the paste to the affected areas. The paste has a bite or sting to it but it does kill the bacteria in the infection.

OTHER USES

Mountain bush pepper has a strong earthy flavour with a hint of heat. You can add ground mountain bush pepper leaf to olive oil for dressings and tapas platters. It adds a unique flavour to dukkah, and also any roasted meats or vegetables. A small bowl of ground mountain bush pepper placed in the centre of the table can be 'pinched' over soups and sauces, much like black pepper.

FRUIT

Native almonds, beach almonds

ABORIGINAL NAME/S

Unknown

BOTANICAL NAME

Terminalia catappa

Native almonds are a large-growing, tropical tree from the leadwood tree family. They are native to other countries such as Africa, Asia, the Pacific, Madagascar and Seychelles. People commonly know these beach trees as sea almonds, beach almond tree or tropical almond trees.

These trees grow locally along the North Queensland coastline; they are one of the few coastal trees which lose their leaves between June and August. Commonly by the end of August all their leaves have turned a deep red and have fallen, covering the ground with layers of red, orange and brown foliage. The leaves, which are oval shaped, glossy dark green and leathery looking, grow from 15 to 25cm long and 10 to 14cm wide.

By September, new green shoots will start to form and by November, the trees will be in full green fruit. The fruits, like the leaves, also change colours from green, yellow, orange to red, then a deep purple colour when they have ripened. The fruit contains an almond seed, which is edible, and is known to have medicinal properties. It's a favourite food for cassowary and fruit bats. The flesh is tough to separate from the hard stone but can be eaten raw; it tastes slightly bitter with a distinctive tart flavour. The smooth outer skin covers an inner layer of corky fibres which surround the nut and help the fruit to float.

These trees grow in various sizes, up to 35-50m tall, with horizontal branches that are mostly arranged in distinctive tiers. A beautiful well-supported tree has an alluring canopy, which is unique in the tree world, and is one of the great characteristics to this incredible tropical tree. It requires a fair amount of space. As the tree ages the canopy grows into an umbrella-like shape, with a thick, lush spreading form that creates shade during summer.

TRADITIONAL USE

The nuts hold a high amount of nutrients and are harvested when dry. They are either crushed raw to eat the seeds inside or roasted on hot sandy coals to give a nuttier flavour. By roasting the nuts, they release a natural oil which is very filling.

OTHER USES

Extracts from the giant almond leaf reveal significant antibacterial properties, unlike commercially used antibiotics. Other countries around the world such as Mexico, India and South America use these leaves to get rid of intestinal parasites, colic, scabies, skin diseases, coughs, headaches and eye problems, and treat asthma, leprosy, and liver diseases.

The seed can be eaten alone or used for preparing fruit salad, smoothies or for garnishing dishes. Oil, which can be used for cooking, can also be extracted from the dried nuts.

HERB

Native basil

ABORIGINAL NAME/S

Unknown

BOTANICAL NAME

Ocimum tenuiflorum

Native basil is an aromatic plant, which grows wild on rocky ledges and rugged surfaces in the dry and hot climate of Queensland and the Northern Territory.

Native basil is an ankle-high, woody herb with small, pale-green, pointed leaves that are 3–5cm long. The plant has soft, delicate, fragrant, lush foliage that is extremely hardy, so it grows well through summer and throughout the year in warmer areas of Australia. The plant can be mistaken for a weed, but if you crush the leaves in your hand you will be able to distinguish if it is native basil by its woody–sweet basil scent.

TRADITIONAL USE

Aboriginal Australians use this plant for medicinal and ceremonial purposes. For medicinal purposes, the leaves are crushed into a paste and applied to infected wounds, boils and on skin infections until they dry up. It also works as a painkiller and can be used to fight off infections as it contains traces of antibacterial properties. In ceremony, the dried leaves and branches are used in a smoking ceremony by adding them to hot coals to create a smoke used to cleanse bodies or places of bad energies.

Traditionally, women would also use native basil as a form of perfume. They would lightly crush the leaves to release the sweet aromas and then rub the paste on their bodies and through their hair to smell sweet.

OTHER USES

Native basil can be used in the same way as Asian or sweet basil. It is a great base for many dishes including pesto sauce, which is a combination of garlic, olive oil, pine nuts, basil and shavings of parmesan cheese. You can also add native basil to your pasta dishes, and your Asian dishes such as stir-fries or curries.

FRUIT

Native finger lime

ABORIGINAL NAME/S

Unknown

BOTANICAL NAME

Citrus australasica

Native finger limes are another little treat that the Australian bush produces. A mature tree can grow about 6–10m high. The small tree is now native only to rainforest areas of south-east Queensland and northern New South Wales, as its habitat has been destroyed by farming and commercial land developments.

Finger limes are a treasure to local Aboriginal People and other Australians who know about them, but in the past decade the demand for finger limes has grown steadily because they have been discovered on a grander scale.

They are now being heavily promoted in commercial kitchens around Australia and the world as citrus caviar, citrus gems and citrus pearl drops.

The finger lime tree is spindly and quite spikey. The leaves are small, dark green, shiny and delicate, and can grow from 1 to 2cm long and half a centimetre thick. The tree is deeply layered with thorns, which grow to about 3cm long, longer than the leaves.

Native finger limes grow in the shape of fingers, hence their name. On average, a healthy finger lime can grow as long as 6–12cm and as thick as 2cm. The lime's pulp comes in an assortment of colours from lime to dark green, bright to light pink, blood orange to light orange, and to pearly yellows. You can generally tell the juice colour from the colour of the skin.

The delicate flowers are small and white, and have a sweet scent. The tree starts flowering from June to early October, but in warmer climates the tree may flower sporadically throughout spring and summer. Fruit development can last as long as five months from flowering to harvesting, with the fruit maturing between December and May.

TRADITIONAL USE

Finger limes have been a food source for Aboriginal Australians for thousands of years. They are also used to fight off any viral or bacterial diseases. Finger limes can be used as an antiseptic for infected sores or boils by crushing the pulp and applying the juice to the wounds.

OTHER USES

Finger limes are highly sought after by chefs in commercial kitchens and restaurants all over the world. These citrus gems are not only used in sweet and savoury Australian dishes, but infusing finger limes into Asian cooking has become a huge trend over the last few years.

Finger limes have become increasingly popular in chutneys, jams, marmalades, marinades, and savoury and citrus sauces. They are also used as a garnish, especially for beverages such as champagne and cocktails.

Finger limes are ideal with fish (raw or cooked), oysters, chicken, pork and salads. They are best eaten fresh but can be frozen to use later.

Native gooseberry

ABORIGINAL NAME/S

Unknown

BOTANICAL NAME

Physalis minima

Gooseberry shrubs are often found in dry soil in areas near water systems such as riverbanks, on the edges of swampy areas and, most often, around cattle yards (post-colonisation). They grow in the Kimberley region in Western Australia, Arnhem Land in the Northern Territory, and in the Cape York region in Far North Queensland.

The shrubs look very spindly, with bright, dark-green leaves and small, delicate, white flowers. They can grow as high as 1–2m. Each shrub has hundreds of small, paper-thin pods which change from green to a golden-yellow colour when they ripen. As the fruit ripens inside the paper-thin pod, the pod will change from soft and moist to brown and dry, with a crepe paper–like texture. When it ripens and turns yellow, the pod, with the fruit inside, will fall to the ground. Inside the paper-thin pod is a small tomato-like fruit. Growing 1–2cm in length, the fruit, like the pod, changes from green to a bright-yellow colour as it ripens. The fruit matures between December and February.

TRADITIONAL USE

Aboriginal People still collect gooseberries in the wild today. They are a popular delicacy, especially women and children who will spend hours sitting in one spot collecting buckets and buckets of fresh gooseberries from shrubs and from the ground.

OTHER USES

Gooseberries are delicious eaten raw. They are sweet and taste very similar to a cherry tomato, with a slightly tangier aftertaste. These little berries are known to contain high levels of vitamin C.

Gooseberries all around the world have been a popular fruit in home kitchens. They are great in pies, salads and tarts; gooseberry jams are a personal favourite. They can also be dried out and then crushed into a powder which is lovely to add to marinades and savoury, meaty dishes like stews and barbecue meats, or you can use it with seafood.

Native Australian gooseberries are also making their way into commercial kitchens in Australia. They're used mainly in desserts and work particularly well with other berries (including strawberries), apples and melted dipping chocolate.

Native guava

ABORIGINAL NAME/S

bolwarra
Dharawal tribe, formerly of coastal area now known as the Sydney basin, NSW

BOTANICAL NAME

Eupomatia laurina

Native guava is a large spreading shrub growing 3–5m high. It has multiple trunks and glossy, dark green leaves which grow between 6 and 12cm long, on 1cm-thick vine-like branches. In the cooler winter and spring weather, the foliage takes on a red–bronze colour. It grows well in the coastal rainforests of Far North Queensland and as far south as Victoria.

Flowering begins in spring and summer with lily-like flowers, 2.5cm in diameter, producing a sweet scent. However, each flower only lasts one day. The bud of the flower has a pointy cap, exactly like a eucalyptus bud. The flowers are pollinated by small brown weevils, which are attracted to the sweet scent.

The fruit is green in colour and grows in an urn shape, 2–3cm in size. The fruit ripens in winter and is ready when it is soft to squeeze. The creamy pulp is edible and very sweet; it has lots of seeds just like a guava.

TRADITIONAL USE

Aboriginal rainforest people use the native guava leaves to treat diarrhoea, sore throats, vomiting, stomach issues and menstrual pains by simply boiling the leaves and drinking the liquid. The leaves are also used as an antiseptic on inflamed wounds or sores.

OTHER USES

Native guavas are used in savoury and sweet dishes in commercial kitchens. They are also a favourite in the common household and are used in jams, chutneys and even for juicing.

You can buy guava leaf extracts and essential oils to alleviate inflammation and candida, and to assist in fighting germs and infections.

Old man saltbush, saltbush

ABORIGINAL NAME/S

purngep, pining and binga
Noongar tribe, WA

BOTANICAL NAME

Atriplex nummularia

With its silver-grey foliage, saltbush is a unique, fast-growing shrub that grows to 1–3m tall and from 2 to 5m in width. This shrub is highly ornamental and is often used as hedging or screening as it offers a unique contrast in colour against other green plants in a garden. It also presents a thick foliage, with leaves that are rough in texture, with a scaly coating and crinkled edges. This species grows in all parts of Australia in arid to subtropical environments with cool to warm temperatures.

The saltbush plant has high resistance to drought and sandy soil; in the wild, juvenile plants will struggle to establish in conditions that are too dry and barren. The small flowers are male and female, borne on different plants. The female flowers grow in dense clusters, approximately 20cm long, while the male flowers are globular, crowding along the ends of each branch.

The foliage is elliptical to circular-shaped, with wavy margins, varying in different sizes. The leaves grow to 2–3cm but will grow larger and more vegetable-like in hotter conditions. Saltbush will grow well in the ground or in small pots, if harvested frequently. It makes great space filler in garden beds, but as it will grow as a sprawling specimen, it will require regular pruning.

The great thing about this plant is that the leaves can be harvested year-round for diverse culinary use. It's perfect for imparting a strong salty flavour to salads and savoury dishes. The leaves and the seeds are a sustainable food source, adding a rich salty flavour, as well a high source of minerals such as antioxidants and protein to every dish.

TRADITIONAL USE

Saltbush is used by Aboriginal People to treat wounds, sores and burns. It is crushed up into a paste with water and applied on the infected area.

OTHER USES

Old man saltbush can easily be introduced into your kitchen just as one would commonly use salt and pepper. Adding this native herb to one or two of your dishes will not only make your food taste delicious, but is a great way to create a unique and memorable dish for a dinner party or event.

Pandanus

ABORIGINAL NAME/S

wa-wirdiwirdi
Yanyuwa tribe, Borroloola Gulf of Carpentaria, NT

tiungal or win-nam
Kabi Kabi tribe, Sunshine Coast, Queensland

BOTANICAL NAME

Pandanus spiralis and Pandanus tectorius

Pandanus palms are versatile plants that have many uses to Aboriginal People in Australia. The plants not only offer food, but also natural fibres suitable for many types of weaving. Pandanus palms grow well in the northern parts of Australia, as well as the low islands of Polynesia, Micronesia, and Melanesia.

There are approximately 30 species of pandanus growing in Australia, though they are a genus of over 600 worldwide species. They are generally found in tropical and subtropical terrains, and warm climate areas where frost is not a problem. They prefer to grow in well-drained soils, in a sunny location and are tolerant of exposed coastal situations. Tough and hardy plants, they can withstand drought, strong winds and salt spray, but need a freshwater source to draw from. You'll find them in open woodlands, coastlines, lagoons, mangrove fringes, lowline swamps, and along river banks. Other pandanus species are adapted to mountain habitats and riverine forests where they may be understorey shrubs.

Also known as a screw pine, pandanus commonly grow with a broad canopy and heavy fruit pods. Depending on the species and terrain, pandanus can represent a diversity of growth forms such as shrubs and trees. Mature trees can reach up to 10-20m tall, with leaves spanning 5m in length or longer. As shrubs they are a low-line type, less than 1-2m tall, covering the ground, draping and clustering over each other.

These trees have an almost mystic appearance, as their root systems form and grow off the trunk into the ground in a triangular, or pyramid shape, which provides a support or anchoring system for the top-heavy tree. A fully grown pandanus can have many branches, with a smooth trunk and rough, wart-like growths all over the trunks.

They produce a bountiful, large seed pod from June to October. These pods turn bright orange as they ripen and are a favourite food of sulphur-crested cockatoos. The fruits can stay on the tree for more than 12 months, but when they fall to the ground, the seed pods detach from the core of the fruit and the seeds crumble into individual parts. The edible part of the seeds is the kernel inside the seed, which can only be eaten once they are roasted in hot coals. The flowers grow in clusters, surrounded by large bracts, and will appear throughout the year.

TRADITIONAL USE

Over time, Aboriginal People have found many uses for the pandanus plant. The most obvious use of pandanus is as an easy source of bush tukka; not many people know that the white-growing bases of the leaves are edible and easy to access. They taste similar to cabbage or silver beet; they can be eaten raw or cooked and offer highly nutritional fibres.

As for the fruit pods, they separate into small blocks, with each wedge housing several small, almond-like kernel nuts. The fruit wedges are tough and fibrous, but, depending on species, sometimes the base of the packed wedges is soft enough to chew or suck on to extract some pulp, which can be sweet or bitter. The fruit core itself, which the wedges attach to, is also edible, although it is usually very woody and tasteless.

Aboriginal People from across Arnhem Land still utilise the pandanus leaves today. They have moved into more modern methods of harvesting, dyeing and weaving pandanus baskets and ornaments. The production of such products has created employment opportunities by offering workshops and tours that take people out onto Country to learn how to collect materials and create hand-woven baskets and jewellery.

Medicinally, the use of pandanus trees is common amongst many Aboriginal tribes. The Bininj/Mungguy freshwater people from central Arnhem Land have mastered the use of the pandanus trunk to treat stomach pain, diarrhoea and wounds. The young sprouts are pounded down into a paste to use as an antiseptic ointment and to aid toothaches, mouth sores and ulcers.

FRUIT

Pigface

ABORIGINAL NAME/S

karkalla, bain
Noongar tribe, WA

janga
Wajarri tribe, WA

pigface kanikung/canajong
palawa tribe, Tasmania

BOTANICAL NAME

Carpobrotus rossii

Pigface is also well known as noon flower, ice plant and cutwort. This special plant is very difficult to write about as it has so many amazing features to explore. With its stunning green, plump, succulent leaves and the contrast of the bright vibrant pink flowers, it looks beautiful as ground cover over

FRUIT

the sand dunes. When it fruits, it offers so many health and culinary benefits. The pigface fruit has a delicious salty but sweet flavour, with lots of flesh and seeds inside and is highly sought after in the culinary world as it can be used in jams, chutneys and syrups. The leaves can be used in a medicinal way to heal burns, cuts and open wounds.

Pigface is part of the Aizoaceae or stone plants family and is native to South Africa and Australia. It grows in Queensland, New South Wales, Western Australia, South Australia, Tasmania and Victoria. It can be observed year-round as large patches of ground cover along sand dunes, close coastal limestone escarpments, and other coastline areas. Pigface grows low to the ground, barely reaching 0.5m in height, but can spread as wide as 3m.

It will produce bright pink and purple flowers in spring and summer. Flowering starts through August to October. Flowers grow to 3.5-5.5cm in diameter, with layers of long, ribbon-like petals about 4-5cm long with a beautiful yellow centre. The succulent leaves are long, plump and firm, triangular-shaped and blue-green in colour. Poking up from the soil, they are thick and have a clear, jelly-like texture inside, very similar to aloe vera, though not slimy.

The fruit ripens when the flower is pollinated and remains on the stem after the flower dries up and falls off. The fig-like fruit will turn a deep pink, to red colour. It's the size of a red grape, so you can easily find them amongst the green ground-cover foliage. The fruit can be eaten fresh: just hold one end and suck out the sweet pulp or eat it whole – it has a delicious salty skin. Inside the leathery skin is a soft gooey texture with a large number of small seeds, similar to a dragon fruit, and holds a similar bland flavour. If eaten with the outer layer of the skin, it will give you a saltier flavour.

I know what you're thinking by now, it's a weird name for a bush fruit – but the name pigface is derived from two things: some say the fruit resembles a pig's face and others will say the fruit are in the shape of a pig. Please don't let the name deter you from trying it because there is so much to enjoy about this incredible plant and fruit.

TRADITIONAL USE

It is widely used for food and to treat ailments by many Aboriginal People. They will eat the fruit, either fresh or sun-dried. The salty leaves were also reported to have been eaten with meat after roasting them on the hot coals.

Aboriginal People knew there were many health benefits in eating this plant, without knowing the scientific information. The succulent leaves are used to treat sores, infections and burns by applying the juice of the leaf to the infected areas (very similar to how aloe vera leaves are used). Extracts of the plant have been found to have antioxidant, antiplatelet, and anti-inflammatory activity. It is also used as a hydrating supplement if fresh water isn't available.

OTHER USES

Nowadays, this incredible plant and its fruit are taking the culinary market by storm. There are many wild harvest businesses selling the fruit commercially to be turned into gourmet jams, chutneys, jellies and cakes, or paired with seafood in savoury dishes.

The leaves can be eaten raw or cooked like a vegetable, as well as used like aloe vera to remedy stings, burns and skin irritations.

FRUIT

Rainforest tamarind

ABORIGINAL NAME/S

biliybiliy
Djabugay tribe, Kuranda, Far North Queensland

BOTANICAL NAME

Diploglottis smithii

Rainforest tamarind is a thin tree growing to a height of 15–20m. It is native to south-eastern Queensland and northern New South Wales, and occurs naturally in wet, tropical rainforests. These trees can still be found growing in the wild, along coastal lowland around the north coast of New South Wales and on the Sunshine Coast and the Gold Coast hinterland in Queensland.

Native tamarinds are related to the Asian lychee family but certainly don't taste like lychees. Despite its name, the native tamarind is also not at all related to the common tamarind. It is a tall tree with large, rounded, green leaves, which are almost leathery or waxy-looking. The rainforest tamarind flowers in summer, producing small, delicate, creamy flowers.

The fruit grows in clusters and is ready to harvest in autumn. It hangs gracefully in a light-brown casing, holding three vibrant-red seeds. Its flesh is sour and tangy, very similar in flavour to green mango.

TRADITIONAL USE

Aboriginal People gather the native tamarinds every year. They offer a delicious treat for the men, women and children as they eat them raw.

Traditionally, women and children would sit by a river or creek and crush the fruit off the seeds. Then they would add water to the crushed fruit, creating a refreshing, tasty beverage.

OTHER USES

Just like common tamarind, native tamarind can be made into jams, chutneys and sauces for savoury, sour and sweet dishes. Native tamarind works well with chicken, pork, lamb and beef, especially in Indian and Asian dishes like curries, stews and stir-fries. The tangy, sour flavour can also work extremely well in baked dishes such as cheesecakes, biscuits and slices. It also makes refreshing cordial.

Native tamarind is full of vitamin C and natural minerals, offering a great way to boost your immune system.

HERB

Red back ginger

ABORIGINAL NAME/S

Unknown

BOTANICAL NAME

Alpinia caerulea

You really cannot mistake the red back ginger, with its vibrant blue berries. Commonly known as native ginger, it's a subspecies of the Atherton Tableland red back ginger. This scruffy-looking plant is a recurring herb which grows extremely well under the rainforest canopy of the wet tropics throughout eastern Australia. It can be found in fringes of coastal rainforests from north of Sydney to as far as Cape York in Far North Queensland regions.

Native ginger is an easy-growing plant and great to use in landscaping as it's an attractive-looking plant and fills a ground area of between 3-5m, growing as tall as 2m in height. The leaves are glossy, dark green in colour and will grow in a long, thick, blade-looking shape. The plant bears a stalk of white flowers which has a beautiful sweet fragrance. It will flower in spring and summer, then bears a small, round, deep-blue fruit that stays on the plant for several months. Each fruit is around 10-18mm wide and has an egg-like casing which hides a mass of black seeds, surrounded by a white pulp which can be eaten. You'll taste a slight gingery-lemon flavour.

TRADITIONAL USE

Aboriginal tribes from coastal areas traditionally ate the roots as well as the young shoots and often used the flesh around the seeds to encourage salivation while walking through the forest. It is said that the pathways of these Peoples could be detected by the trail of discarded seeds and growth over the years.

OTHER USES

The ground roots and the berries can be used to make delicious teas. Because this is a root, it is a close relative of edible cardamom, ginger, turmeric and galangal. Some people plant these in their gardens as an attractive and useful native bush food plant that grows well in shady moist ground.

Riberry

ABORIGINAL NAME/S

Unknown

BOTANICAL NAME

Syzygium luehmannii

I have included this lilly pilly due to the amount of people who ask if these berries are edible. My answer is – Yes!

Riberry is a medium-sized, coastal rainforest tree. Common names include riberry, small-leaved lilly pilly, native berries or clove lilli pilli. This beautiful shrub-like plant is actually related to the clove tree, from Indonesia. The natural habitat for this species is around riverine, coastal shoreline, subtropical or tropical rainforest. It grows on volcanic soils or deep sandy soils, between northern parts of New South Wales to Far North Queensland.

The plant flowers from September through to October, with flowers that are white or cream and form in bunches of four to five. The fruits form from October to March. Whilst they are very similar in shape to a blueberry, the riberries are a lot tarter in flavour- cranberry-like, with a hint of clove. The fruit has been known to contain high levels of vitamin C and is rich in nutritional value, such as antioxidants and fibre. As the berries grow in tight, abundant clusters at the ends of each twig, it makes them perfect for picking.

Riberries grow small, glossy, spearhead-shaped leaves which are a dark, shiny green when mature. But the beautiful thing about this plant is the pink–red colour of the new leaf growth; this is what attracts many people to buy them for hedging.

TRADITIONAL USE

Riberries are popular as a super bush food, offering a high level of vitamin C and antioxidants. They have been used for thousands of years by Aboriginal People as a natural source of hydration. They are also used as a natural antiseptic to treat sores and infections. After crushing the berries and adding some water, the liquid can be placed on the infected wounds.

OTHER USES

The tart, slightly spicy fruit is used to make uniquely flavoured jams, preserves, sauces, syrups and confectionery. It can also be eaten and enjoyed straight off the tree. The riberry is also very popular as a garden ornamental and street tree. It is easily maintained as a smaller tree through light pruning and is easy to shape and maintain.

Rose apple, malabar plum

ABORIGINAL NAME/S

Unknown

BOTANICAL NAME

Syzygium jambos

This beautiful pale-yellow fruit, commonly known as rose apple or malabar plum, belongs to the Myrtaceae or the myrtle family. These tropical, exotic fruits have many different varieties, which have naturalised throughout the tropical and subtropical regions of the world and appear with many shades of colours from green, red, plum-rose and yellow. This particular species is introduced and was actually native to south-east Asia, but has been included here due to its popularity in many communities.

These small, oval-shaped fruits grow on a relatively large, wide, spreading tree, or a small- to medium-sized shrub, growing anywhere from 3 to 15m in height. They are commonly used as ornamental trees, great for shielding from the elements and providing thick shade. The natural design of the tree is low branching, with leaves that are long and slender, growing about 2-4cm in width and 10-20cm long, with a wedge-shaped base and pointed end. The leaves start with a vibrant red colour when growing, but turn to dark, glossy green when full sized.

The flowers are small pom pom–like clusters, with white or pale green long stamens, blossoming to approximately 5–8cm in diameter. The rose apple will usually flower during the summer months, with the fruits to follow around four months later.

The fruits grow to approximately 2-5cm in diameter. At the base of the fruit are four green petals, otherwise known as sepals. The small round apples ripen from green to a stunning pale yellow once matured. The is skin is very smooth and waxy in appearance, and look like small Christmas ornaments. They are called 'rose' because when you eat the fruit, it has a sweet, candy, rose-like scent to it. Under the surface of the flesh is usually white or sometimes pale yellow or brown. It has a fibrous spongy texture and looks very similar to a guava fruit, though somewhat smoother. You would think when bitten into, it would be juicy and loaded with seeds, like a guava, but instead it has between one and four large brown seeds that detach from the semi-dry flesh of the fruit once it has ripened.

TRADITIONAL USE

Aboriginal People eat these fruits raw. They are a nice sweet treat, and particularly popular with women and children.

OTHER USES

Due to their delicate nature, rose apples are not commercially cultivated. They can bruise easily and have a short shelf-life once picked, making it difficult for them to viable in commercial marketplaces. However, people still wild harvest them for desserts, cordials, salads and preserves.

The fruits are a good source of vitamins A and C, are full of antioxidants and can help reduce inflammation in the immune system. They are also high in fibre, potassium, magnesium, iron and small amounts of calcium.

FRUIT

Sandpaper fig

ABORIGINAL NAME/S

yanggi
Djabugay tribe, Kuranda, Far North Queensland

BOTANICAL NAME

Ficus fraseri

The hardy sandpaper fig trees are looked upon as a weed, but to the ecosystem in which they live, these trees serve as an important food source for birds, caterpillars, butterflies, fruit bats, flying foxes and many other animals. These trees grow well in a warm, dry climate around water systems, riverbanks, rainforests and creeks. They are found in the northern parts of Australia and along the east coast from Mackay in Queensland, through New South Wales and just into Victoria near Mallacoota. A mature tree can reach about 8m high, but along coastal edges the trees grow quite small, about

2–4m, due to the high winds off the coast. The sandpaper fig flowers and fruits from spring to early summer and the fruit matures from December to February.

The name 'sandpaper fig' comes from the texture of the leaves, which are rough and harsh – exactly like sandpaper. The fruit are small, round and fig-like. They go from green to a deep-maroon colour when ripe, growing to about 1–2cm, with light, short hairs on the outer layer.

The fruit is sweet and moist with hundreds of little brown seeds. Like a fig, the outer layer is soft and sweet, and the tiny hairs on the outer layer are fine to eat. The leaves are dark green and grow to about 5–15cm long.

TRADITIONAL USE

The local Aboriginal People commonly consume sandpaper figs as they are a sweet, nutritional treat. But traditionally, the tree was more than just a food source. The men used the leaves to sand back their tools and weapons, such as boomerangs, spears, coolamons and axe handles, to a smooth surface.

The thick, white tree sap was, and still is, used to treat the itchy symptoms and skin infections of ringworm by applying a thin layer over the ringworm scars.

OTHER USES

Sandpaper figs are sometimes found on menus in commercial restaurants, served up as delicious desserts, cooked in the way that common figs are: roasted, baked or pan-fried in butter and syrup.

GRASS

Spiny-head mat rush, basket grass

ABORIGINAL NAME/S

jikan
Kuku Yalanji tribe, Far North Queensland

BOTANICAL NAME

Lomandra longifolia

Lomandra is a common grass that grows in clumps, mostly around all parts of Australia, except for Northern Territory and Western Australia. You'll often find it in sandy soils around swamps and wet places, like the banks of rivers and creeks, hillsides, cliffs and around open forests. It's an evergreen, perennial herb.

This clumpy grass is also used as an ornamental plant in gardens, as it grows well with little to no maintenance required. The long, blade-like leaves can grow between 40 and 120cm long, and 5 to 10 mm wide. The leaves have sharp, slender edges and must be handled carefully as they can cause cuts.

The flowers of lomandra are pale yellow in colour and appear as a long cluster of stems, which have smaller clusters of cream, or yellow, stalkless flowers at the end. The flowers themselves are small and seed-like, growing 2–4mm long; they give off an incredible sweet, heavy scent in warm temperatures from late winter to early spring. The uniqueness of the cluster flower head is that it is actually a seed capsule.

Lomandra can be seen in many commercial and private gardens, often grown because of its hardiness.

TRADITIONAL USE

This plant is very versatile for Aboriginal People; they use the leaves of lomandra to make woven baskets and mats. The white ends of the leaves can be chewed to suck out the moisture for hydration. It also is a great source of fibre and vitamins, with a sweet taste and crunchy texture, like the stem of bok choy.

Traditionally, the women were the ones who used the grass mostly. They would gather the young leaves from the middle of the clusters as they were easy to pull out and softer to split each blade into thin straps with their finger nails to start the weaving process. They mastered the artform of basketry to use as mats and fish traps. Because of the strong durability of the fibres, they last a very long time in and out of the water. The grass also makes strong ropes, used with weaponry and basket carrying.

The seeds were and are still being used to make flour or eaten just for the fibre. They can be eaten raw, straight from the plant, which tastes very fibrous and chewy, but has quite a woody, tangy taste.

To harvest the seeds, the women collect and dry them in the sun, then they smash it on the rocks to get the seeds off the stem. The seeds could then be roasted on hot rocks, then crushed to separate the husk from the seeds. They would be dried again and then ground into a fine powder. Often, water was added to the flour to make a batter for patties, cooked over the hot coals. It's a long process which could now be made quicker with modern equipment, but back in those days, they knew how to control the process well.

OTHER USES

This plant is now used to make jewellery and high-end fashionable art clothing by Aboriginal artists across the country.

Sugarleaf

ABORIGINAL NAME/S

Unknown

SCIENTIFIC NAME

Glycaspis (Glycaspis) brimblecombei

Sugarleaf are lerps, which are tiny, white, transparent shells or sometimes little fluff balls about 2–4mm long. These sweet white lerps are produced predominantly on eucalypt leaves by tiny, yellow, sap-sucking psyllid beetles, which use the lerps or droplets for protection. The sugarleaf are essentially made of sugars and starches extracted from the sap and expelled by the bugs. If you look closely at the white shells you will notice a similarity to fairy floss, and you will see the minuscule insects that are responsible for producing these little sweet sugar droplets. Sugarleaf can be found on gum trees and grey ironbark leaves, usually close to riverbanks.

They are produced at the end of the dry season, just before the wet season.

These lerps are also referred to as 'sugar bread' and are eaten by simply running the leaf between your teeth; don't worry about eating the insects, you don't really taste them.

TRADITIONAL USE

Aboriginal People really enjoyed eating sugarleaf, and they continue to enjoy them today. Children would collect and indulge in these sweet treats in between playing in their local waterholes.

OTHER USES

The old people in the East Kimberley used sugarleaf to sweeten their tea. They would gather a whole branch and shake it onto a sheet to gather the sugarleaf.

HERB

Warrigal greens

ABORIGINAL NAME/S

warrigal
Wiradjuri tribe, central NSW

BOTANICAL NAME

Tetragonia tetragonoides

This gorgeous plant, well known as warrigal greens, is one of my favourites as it's an edible succulent and a remarkably diverse plant. Native to the southern Australian coastline, it offers a lot of healthy nutritional properties, often being described as native spinach. This hardy little plant grows in all types of soils and is tolerant of wind and full sun exposure, as well as lightly shaded environments. Growing close to the ground, it can be found between rocks near beaches and in sand dunes around estuaries as it thrives in wind and on salty soil. This little bush grows layers upon layers of lush, green, spear-shaped leaves.

HERB

Warrigal greens is a member of the Aizoaceae family and is related to figs and marigolds. It is also native to other countries, such as New Zealand, parts of eastern Asia and around the Pacific Rim. In some places, they refer to this plant as the New Zealand spinach or Botany Bay spinach, but in the Wiradjuri language it's called warrigal, which means 'wild dog', as the ten-sided seed looks like a dog's face when dry.

This native plant grows quickly, reaching 2m in width and 30cm in height. It can be grown in apartments or on balconies. Most nurseries around the southern parts of Australia now sell this plant. If you are brave enough to grow the Warrigal spinach, it is recommended to keep the seeds and dry them out to plant in the next spring.

TRADITIONAL USE

Aboriginal People eat warrigal greens to settle bad tummy aches, as well as for hydration. It has high levels of vitamins K, C and B6, not to mention manganese. **NOTE: Due to the high levels of oxalic acid, the leaves need pre-treatment or heating before eating. The best way to do this is blanching or boiling them in hot water for 10–15 seconds, then drain well before using in your cooking.**

OTHER USES

To add to your everyday cooking, fold into omelettes or use them to make a delicious pesto.

FLOWER

Waterlily

ABORIGINAL NAME/S

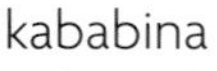

kababina
Kuku Yalanji tribe, Far North Queensland

BOTANICAL NAME

Nymphaea violacea

These majestic waterlilies are very sacred flowers. Waterlily predominately grow in tropical wetlands. They grow from either rhizomes or tubers. The native Australian waterlily is also known as the blue lotus, and can be seen in many water channels across New South Wales and Queensland. These enchanting waterlilies come in different shades of white, pink, red, apricot and yellow.

The uniqueness of waterlilies is that they are floating aquatic plants that grow best in slow-moving water or lakes, ponds, billabongs, swamps and still rivers or creeks. Their roots can settle in silt and do not have to be buried deep but, waterlilies do require a lot of sun to grow and produce their breathtaking flowers.

Waterlilies, come in two distinctive types- the hardy varieties, which grow extremely well in most climates, and the tropical waterlilies, which thrive in subtropical to warm conditions, more in the northern regions of Australia from the western Northern Territory to Far North Queensland and northern New South Wales.

All plants of the *Nymphaea* are aquatic. They are attached to a long stem or petioles that is hollow, spongy and fibrous inside, filled with gases to help get the expanding leaf to the surface of the water. The top of the stem is the thin, flat waxy round heart shaped leaf, otherwise known as the 'lilly pad'; the pad absorbs the sunlight to make nutrients to feed the rhizome down below in the water. The leaves are just as majestic as the flower, round or oval-shaped with a perfect split called a sinus that travels to the centre of the lily pad. Some of the pads will have a spread of brown, red or burgundy pigments and rippled edges.

Now for the most beautiful part of this plant, the floating flower or lily. The flowers hauntingly stand above the water's altar. Each flower varies in size, growing to approximately 6–10cm in diameter, but is always identical in looks, a small tear drop bud that opens to the dawning light and during the day. When the flower matures, and closes back up forever, it will sink itself to the bottom of the water and submerge itself in the mud to repeat the germinating cycle.

TRADITIONAL USE

Waterlilies have been a diet staple for many Aboriginal People. They harvest the waterlilies to eat them fresh or roast the bulbs under the hot fire to cook them slightly, which makes the bulb soft warm and gooey. It tastes quite nutty. Full of fibre for Aboriginal Peoples' dietary needs, the bulbs added a yummy, nutty, bitter treat after a swim in the waterholes. They also eat the bottom of the stems which gave them a source of hydration.

When the flowers blossomed, that was a sign that the sugarbag (native honey) was ready to collect. It indicated that the hives in the trees or rock walls would be full of honey from the native bees.

OTHER USES

The waterlily is a spiritual flower in a number of cultures around the world. Many countries have chosen them as the national flower, and many religions often consider waterlilies as a symbolic representation of their beliefs; some of the representations of the lily flower are as a symbol of rebirthing, the new cycle of life, a symbol of unity, universality, enlightenment, passion, love and power. It also can represent knowledge and wisdom, resurrection, chastity and purity, patience, peace, elegance, innocence and a spiritual journey.

SPICE

Wattleseed

ABORIGINAL NAME/S

merne ntange arlepe
Arrernte tribe, central Australia, NT

BOTANICAL NAME

Acacia

Acacias, with their enormous diversity of species and forms, cover the Australian continent. Subsequently, they have been a mainstay in the diet of Aboriginal Australians for thousands of years. **NOTE: Not all acacias are suitable for human consumption – some contain high levels of toxins.**

Wattle trees are shrubby-looking trees, growing as tall as 5–6m. The branches are spindly and covered with spiky thorns up to 1cm long, and long, slender, light-green leaves growing 4–8cm long. Wattles prefer hot and dry temperatures. Because of this, they are mainly harvested in the wild. Hard husks encase the seeds and will last for up to 20 years in their natural environment, usually only germinating after bushfires.

Flowering occurs in August through to December, depending on the region. Each stem holds up to 12 flower-clusters that first appear pale before changing to a vibrant yellow. Seeds are best collected when they are dry and turn dark brown, generally in January, February and March. The seeds were crushed into a powdery consistency between flat grinding stones, and cooked into cakes or damper. Even the green seeds of some species were eaten after baking in the hot coals.

TRADITIONAL USE

Harvested by the Aboriginal People for thousands of years, seeds from wattles were sought out as a versatile and nutritious addition to their diet. Because the hard outer casing protects the seed during long periods of dormancy on the ground, wattleseed has provided Indigenous Australians with a rich source of protein and carbohydrate in times of drought.

Though the plant is a member of the traditionally poisonous *Acacia* genus, Aboriginal People discovered more than 40 different edible varieties. The green seeds are eaten raw, or dried and milled into flour for baking.

Aboriginal People collect the seeds and winnow them from their pods in coolamons or wooden bowls. The seeds can then be ground into a paste and mixed with water to form small, flat cakes. These cakes are baked in the coals of a fire and then eaten or stored for later use. Anyone who has spent time in Australia's deserts will have seen the old grindstones out in the sandhills where Aboriginal women used to sit and prepare their meals. The Aboriginal People also often cooked their food in ovens made by digging a hole in the ground and putting hot coals and hot rocks into it.

OTHER USES

Wattleseed has to be considered the unsung hero of Australian native foods. It is very nutritious, containing potassium, calcium, iron and zinc, all in fairly high concentrations. With a low glycemic index, they are good for diabetics, providing a steady stream of sugars that do not produce sudden rises in blood glucose levels. Wattleseed is very high in protein. Research has been done to investigate the possibilities of Australian wattleseed being used as a famine-relief crop in African countries because it grows in deserts which typically have very poor soil and little or no water.

Today, wattleseed is dried and roasted in a similar way to coffee but with a particular temperature profile. It is then specially ground to produce a highly versatile and nutritious flavour and later crushed to create extracts and a powder used in cooking and for making espresso-type coffee. Described as being reminiscent of hazelnuts and chocolate with hints of coffee, wattleseed is an ideal seasoning for ice-creams, nutty-flavoured butters, sauces and coffee beverages. Roasted ground wattleseed has a diverse number of uses in the kitchen, from baking to a thickening agent for sauces and casseroles. By roasting wattleseed, the most delightful aroma of nutty fresh roasted coffee is released and can be used as a beverage on its own or as an addition to chocolate or desserts. The flowers (without stalks) can also be used, typically in pancakes, scones and scrambled eggs or omelettes, in the same manner as elderberries.

Wattleseed is available online as an extract and a ground spice.

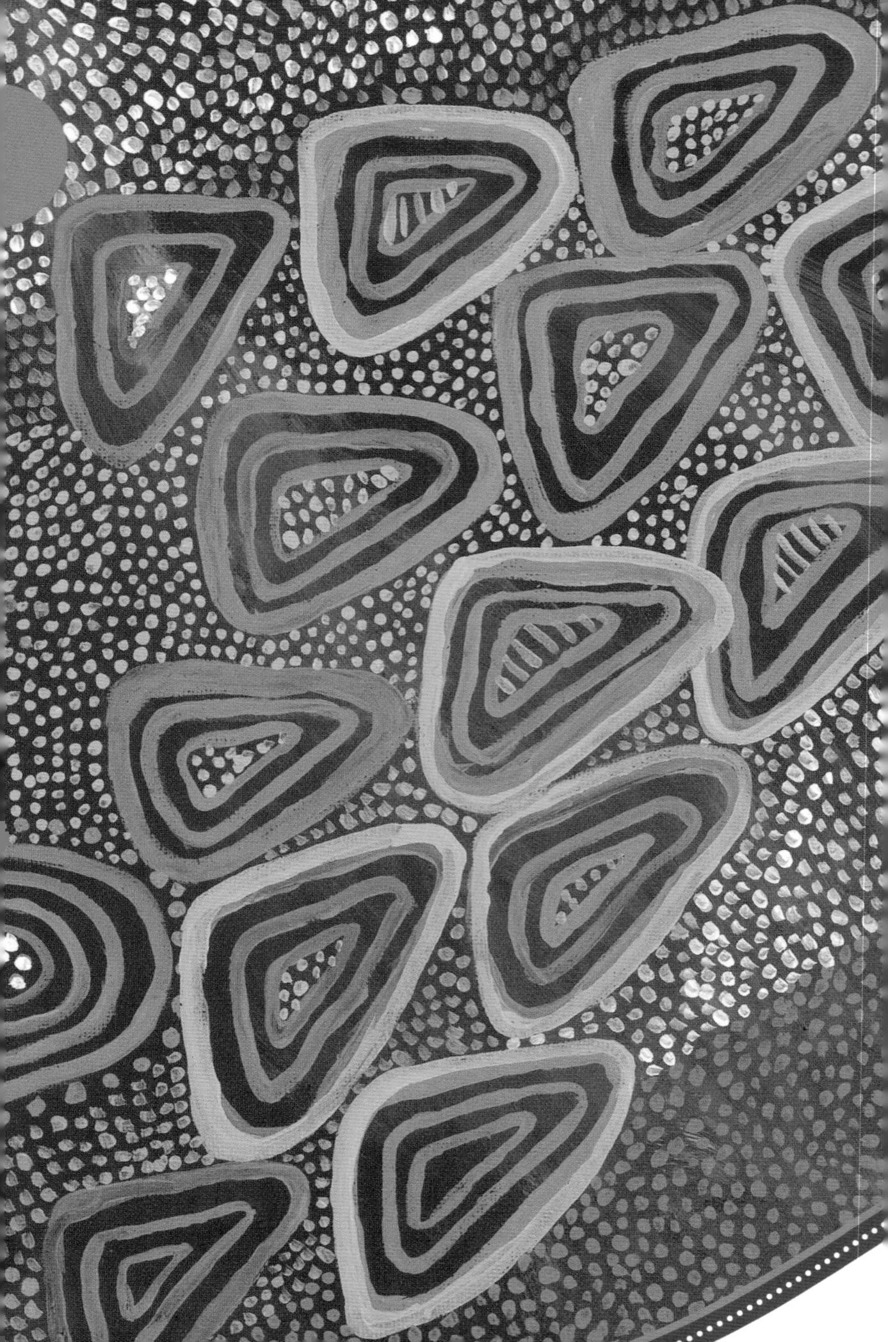

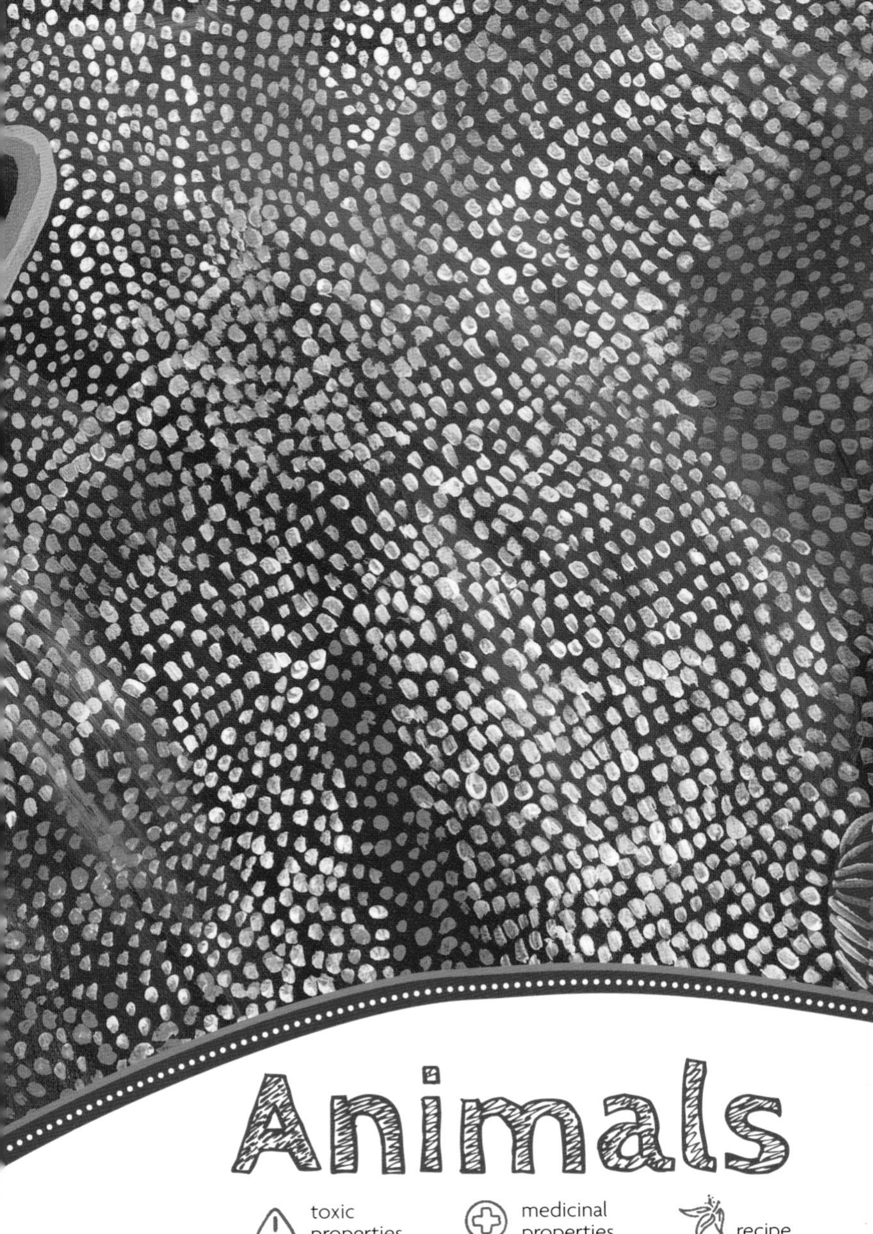

Animals

toxic properties

medicinal properties

recipe

Black bream

ABORIGINAL NAME/S

wulam
Djabugay tribe, Kuranda, Far North Queensland

SCIENTIFIC NAME

Acanthopagrus butcheri

Black bream are a very common fish. Do not mistake it for saltwater sea bream, although they are related. Black bream are golden brown when in the water but their scales turn black once out of the water, which is why they are called black bream. They grow to 60cm long and weigh 4kg on average. They are caught mainly in rivers, creeks and billabongs, but they prefer to swim under overhanging branches among the branches of fallen trees, and in the bottom of deep waterholes.

In summer and early autumn the sperm and eggs are released into the water and the juvenile and adult bream find refuge in the upper level of the estuaries, but they often get washed downstream when the first rains fall in late autumn.

TRADITIONAL USE

Black bream is a treat among Aboriginal People. Small and easy to catch, black bream is often caught and cooked straight out of the water (with scales and guts, so nothing gets wasted) on the coals for 5–10 minutes. Once it's cooked, they just peel the skin off to reveal the white, steaming-hot flesh. It tastes slightly sweet, not to mention it provides a healthy source of protein.

OTHER USES

Bream is becoming as popular as barramundi, but it does not grow as large as barramundi. Black bream fillets are soft and white, and best cooked on hot coals, pan-fried, steamed or poached. Cooking bream whole is the best way to maintain its sweet flavour. It is especially delicious when cooked with Asian flavours.

Bustard bird

ABORIGINAL NAME/S

wawun
Djabugay tribe, Kuranda, Far North Queensland

SCIENTIFIC NAME

Ardeotis australis

Bustard birds, also known as bush turkeys (to Aboriginal People) or plains turkeys, are large ground birds that roam the grasslands, woodlands and open plains, mainly across the northern and central parts of Australia, where the climate is warm and dry.

The bustard bird can grow as tall as 1.5m, and has a wingspan of 2.5m. An average male can weigh 6.5kg. Female birds are smaller and more slender than the males. In appearance, the bustard bird has a mostly dull-brown body and speckles of black and white markings on its wings. Its head is crowned with black feathers and its neck and the bottom half of its body is grey, which helps it blend in with its surroundings.

TRADITIONAL USE

Bustard, or bush turkey as they are some times known (importantly not to be confused with the brush turkey) have played an important role in the diet of Aboriginal People throughout the Kimberley, the central desert, and Far North Queensland. It is still eaten today.

Bustards also play an important part in the Dreaming stories. Many Aboriginal People have totemic spiritual connections with the animal, and are allowed to paint the animals in their art.

As hunters of larger animals, Aboriginal men hunted the bush turkey using weapons like the spear and woomera. The woomera allowed the spear to be thrown faster, harder, more accurately and over longer distances.

When the men brought the bustard back to camp, the women and children were responsible for preparing it for cooking. It was then cooked on the hot coals, allowing the protein, omega fats and oils to remain in the flesh. It can become quite dry or tough in texture if overcooked. The flesh of the turkey is deep red, not white like common turkeys, and the flavour is very gamey.

OTHER USES

Bustard has not yet hit the commercial food industry. In fact, these birds are now protected in some parts of eastern and western Queensland, although Aboriginal People are still allowed to hunt them.

There are various ways to cook bustard. It can be boiled with vegetables and made into a stew. It is especially wonderful when roasted with vegetables for 30–40 minutes (depending on its size). Bustard breasts can also be used in curries or stir-fries, served on a bed of hot rice and vegetables.

REPTILE

Common long-necked turtle

ABORIGINAL NAME/S

min bungarr
Kokoberra tribe, Kowanyama, Cape York Region, Far North Queensland

SCIENTIFIC NAME

Chelodina rugosa

The common long-necked turtle gets its name from its neck, which is sometimes longer than its own body! It can grow up to 25–30cm in length. Its feet are webbed and very strong. It often uses its feet to tear apart its food. This turtle also has a sharp beak and strong jaw, so make sure you keep your fingers away from its beak.

Having dark-brown colouring allows this turtle to hide itself around rocks and mud to escape predators. It also buries itself in mudflats or dried-up riverbeds for protection during the dry season.

Like other reptiles, common long-necked turtles are most active during the dry season, travelling very long distances in search of new waterholes. During winter they lie dormant under logs and rocks, waiting for the water temperature to change before they go in search for food.

In the Kimberley region, there are Kimberley snake-necked turtles, another species of long-necked turtle with the distinguishing feature of having very long chin barbels: thin, thread-like fibres that hang from the bottom of their chins. This is where their tastebuds are located; it helps them search for food in murky waters.

TRADITIONAL USE

Aboriginal People enjoy catching and eating turtle. Aboriginal People in the Kimberley and north-east Arnhem Land prefer to eat turtle than fish, and delight in hunting and feasting on snake-necked turtles, as they are easy to catch in waterholes. When the people in Arnhem Land hunt snake-necked turtles they go to the cracked mudflats and walk along until they see a minuscule bubble amongst the hard, brown, cracked mud. Then they dig until they reach the turtle lying in the damp mud underneath, keeping moist and cool, away from the sun.

Not everyone can eat long-necked turtles. Some people have long-necked turtles as their totemic spiritual symbol. This means that before they were born, their life was of that animal, and they came to be born because their mother ate that animal and embodied its spirit. So to honour the turtle's spirit they must not eat it and if they catch it, they can either pass it onto their grandmothers to eat or let it go.

To cook and prepare a turtle, Aboriginal People will often prepare a fire and let the wood burn down to coals. When the coals are nice and hot, they place the turtle, shell down, to cook the shell through. They do not gut the turtle before cooking it because this ruins the cooking preparation and also lets the juices out. Depending on the heat of the coals and the size of the turtle, it is cooked for 30–40 minutes. They keep a close eye on it to ensure that it does not become overcooked. When holes appear around the legs and the shell, the flesh inside is cooked.

There are two ways to crack open the shell: one is to crack it with a hard object and then approach the meat from the top to the bottom. Alternatively the breast plate is cut away from the shell on the bottom, exposing the legs and guts of the turtle and keeping the juices in the shell.

The flesh of the turtle is pure white and has a similar texture to chicken breast and, in some parts, chicken thighs. But the turtle is much juicer and sweeter in flavour than chicken.

In the past, turtle fats were rubbed on sick or weak babies' chests to give them strength. The oils offered healing minerals. Turtle offered a lot of protein and also gave strength to the men and the old people. Today it is still practised that whenever you catch a turtle, you must give it to the old people first as a sign of respect.

REPTILE

OTHER USES

Turtles don't really get used or cooked in a commercial manner; they are looked upon as more of a bush food that is best cooked in the bush. People in western cultures tend not to eat them because they think that they cannot eat something so cute or, much like whole fish (which many people prefer not to cook because they would rather someone else gut, scale and fillet the fish for them), many people find turtles too difficult to cook.

SHELLFISH

Coorong cockle, Goolwa cockle, or Goolwa pipi

ABORIGINAL NAME/S

bulkiji
Kuku Yalanji tribe, Far North Queensland

SCIENTIFIC NAME

Plebidonax deltoides or *Donax deltoides*

These little shellfish are most commonly known as pipis or clams. They can be found on beaches throughout the eastern parts of Australia and are also prevalent in New Zealand.

Pipis are usually moderately sized, with a strong, durable shell that measures up to 6cm. They have a distinctive wedged shape, with the front edge rounded and the rear side straight.

The outer walls of the shell vary in colour from a beautiful violet to pink, yellow, brown and green. The inner colour is generally white with purple or pink colouring around.

Pipis often appear in large clusters, but populations can be subject to great natural instabilities, causing their numbers to fluctuate. These pipis are an all-time favourite by many and are harvested commercially for both human consumption and bait; at times, they have been considered as a potential species for aquaculture. They are also classified as sea snails and eat plankton or particles in and on the seafloor. Eaten raw, straight out of their shells, the pipi meat is sweet and rubbery; it has a gritty texture due to the sand the pipis absorb from the seafloor. The best way to eat them is to ensure you soak them in salt water to keep them alive and then rinse them in fresh water so they can spit out the sand and clean themselves out.

Pipis can be found on low tide – when the waves wash away, lumps are exposed on the sandy beaches, in low intertidal areas. They burrow shallow in the sand, just below the surface of the water level on the beach and are suspension feeders. They can quickly bury themselves if washed around by the surf.

TRADITIONAL USE

Well, it's not hard to know what and how Aboriginal People use pipis. Most commonly they eat them raw or cook them on hot coals until their shells opened up. They used the shells to make custom jewellery which they could trade, such as head dresses, necklaces and belts. They also used the shells as a knife to cut up other soft foods.

There is evidence to say, that pipis have been an important staple diet for the coastal saltwater people through pipi middens findings, which have been excavated 20kms down through the sand dunes in some coastal areas of northern New South Wales.

OTHER USES

Pipis are now a delicacy in the culinary world and there are thousands of different recipes created with pipis. They have become very commercial and are in high demand in restaurants all over the world. I have added two of my favourite dishes using pipis at the end of the book.

REPTILE

Crocodile

ABORIGINAL NAME/S

baru
Many language groups of Arnhem Land, NT

SCIENTIFIC NAME

Crocodylus porosus (saltwater), *Crocodylus johnstoni* (freshwater)

There are 14 different species of crocodiles that have been identified in the world, but in Australia we have only two: freshwater and saltwater crocodiles.

Freshwater crocodiles are smaller, with a narrow snout; they are light brown with dark markings on the body and tail. They generally live in freshwater habitats, in the warmer waters of the northern parts of Australia, and feed mainly on fish and smaller vertebrates.

The more aggressive crocodiles are the saltwater species, they are the largest living reptiles, with a wider head and a broad rounded snout. The saltwater crocodile is pale yellow and light brown when young, becoming dark green as an adult. Don't be fooled by its name, 'saltwater' crocodile; these giant water reptiles can survive in both fresh and salt water. The male can grow up to 7m long, and can weigh up to 2000kg; the female is generally smaller, reaching 3m in length. They live in mangrove swamps, lagoons, estuaries and low stretches of rivers throughout the northern parts of Western Australia, the Northern Territory and Queensland. So when you're taking a swim or strolling along the far northern beaches or rivers in Australia, be aware and cautious of crocodile-infested waters. Saltwater crocodiles will eat almost anything, from fish, turtles, wild pigs and wallabies to kangaroos, buffalos, dingos, live cattle, dogs and humans.

Saltwater crocodiles are water predators, they stalk their prey by studying their habits and when their prey least expect it, they will go in for the attack. So we encourage you all to abide by the signage- do not risk your own or your pets lives by getting too close to the waters edge.

TRADITIONAL USE

Aboriginal People have been eating crocodile meat for thousands of years. In Arnhem Land they call crocodile 'baru' and there is a strong totemic spiritual connection between the people, the baru and the land, which offers a mutual respect. There are many Dreaming stories from many different language groups around Australia about the crocodile; some tribes in Arnhem Land believe their ancestors crossed swollen rivers on the backs of these people-eaters.

OTHER USES

Crocodiles are being farmed and are sold in leading butchers, commercial meat markets and online, with a wide variety of cuts available. Low in fat and high in protein, the crocodile's white meat is an increasingly popular bush food. It is featured on a lot of restaurant menus around the world. Sourced for its surprisingly tasty, tender flesh, crocodile meat has been used in curries, stir-fries, stews, sausages, pies and casseroles. Crocodile is best cooked medium to guarantee it retains its moisture, otherwise the meat can be tough and chewy. When cooking crocodile, it is best to cook it in the same manner as pork or chicken as they have a similar texture.

Crocodile skin also is highly sought after to use in making handbags, belts, boots and shoes.

MAMMAL

Echidna

ABORIGINAL NAME/S

inape/inarlenge
eastern and central Arrernte language groups, NT

SCIENTIFIC NAME

Tachyglossus aculeatus

About the shape of a football, echidnas are 30–45cm long and can weigh 2–7kg. These unusual-looking, egg-laying mammals are covered with coarse, long, black hair and sharp, yellow, black-tipped needles, which make them very difficult to handle. They have a stubby, hairless tail and long, sharp-clawed feet with which they can burrow through any ground surface, fossicking for food and water. They also find food with their long, sensitive nose. Once they have found food, they use their long, slim, sticky tongue to catch the ants or other insects.

Echidnas are solitary animals. They are always found roaming on their own, but they can be found throughout most of Australia, especially around rocks, hollow logs, termite mounds and holes around tree roots.

TRADITIONAL USE

The Arrernte People of central Australia call the echidna *tjilkamata* and still go hunting for echidna today. Echidnas are very quick on their feet and are fast diggers, so if you find one you have to quickly roll it onto its back so it can't run away.

Before Aboriginal People cook echidna they carefully gut it to remove a poisonous sack, and then, with a skewer, close up the hole. To remove the needles they boil the echidna, then take a strong wire and create a loop around the feet to hold them while they scrape off the needles with a small axe or sharp knife. Once the needles are removed, the echidna is placed on the fire to burn off the remaining coarse hair, before being placed into a camp oven for 2–3 hours, until the meat is cooked right through and is bubbling with juices.

OTHER USES

Echidnas have not hit the commercial markets, because it is seen to be cruel to eat the cute little echidnas, but this cute little animal has been a staple of Aboriginal Peoples' diet for thousands of years and is not hunted in mass numbers. They are also a protected species in some states.

BIRD

Emu

ABORIGINAL NAME/S

karnanganyjal
Jaru tribe, Western Desert, East Kimberley, WA

SCIENTIFIC NAME

Dromaius novaehollandiae

A large flightless bird, standing 2m tall, emus have long, thin necks and soft, brown and grey waterproof feathers. They have light blue skin around their neck, and piecing red eyes. This spectacular bird is related to the ostrich and is recorded as the second largest living bird in the world.

Emus can be found over most of mainland Australia. They prefer to roam around in dry savannah, bushy or scrubby woodlands and very dry areas.

Emus breed in May and June, and a female can mate with several males and lay several batches of eggs in one season. The eggs hatch after approximately eight weeks, and the young chicks are looked after by their fathers. They will reach their full size after six months. An emu can live for up to 10–20 years in the wild, if it survives its predators such as dingos, hawks, eagles and humans.

Emus have strong, leathery feet with three toes and long, strong, black nails. Its nails are one of its only ways to defend itself. Emus have very long legs, allowing them to take a stride of up to 275cm, which makes them extremely fast runners, being able to sprint at 50km per hour.

TRADITIONAL USE

Emus are well-respected birds among Aboriginal People as they represent totems and skin names, and they hold an important place in Australian Aboriginal spirituality. The Yuwaalaraay and other clans around New South Wales say that the spirits created the sun by throwing an emu egg into the sky. The Western Australian Aboriginal People believe that the emu was created when a man was annoying a small bird; the bird threw a boomerang, severing the man's arms and turning him into a flightless emu. The emu was also believed to lie in the Milky Way, high in the sky looking over many Aboriginal language groups.

But in most tribes emu is extremely prized for its meat and feathers, which were traded with other groups. Traditionally, the men hunted larger animals; they had the endurance to walk long distances and the strength to use the weapons like the spear and woomera (a spear throwing device). The men figured out the emu's mating calls and covered themselves in emu feathers to create a coat and used their arms as the neck, to lure the male emus closer before striking them with a spear or axe.

The women worked out that emu fat was good for the skin as a moisturiser, giving it a nice shine, but they also found that it helped to relieve aching bones and joints.

OTHER USES

Emu meat is high in protein and low in fat. It needs to be prepared under strict control to ensure the meat holds its maximum quality. Emu meat is dark red and is best cooked fried or on a hot plate, like a barbecue, to retain its juices and flavour. Emu meat is also best cooked medium–rare, similar to beef, lamb and kangaroo.

Emu oils are also used as a traditional Aboriginal medicine to treat weight loss, stretch marks, dry skin, rashes, eczema, wrinkles and ageing spots and much more. You can purchase the oils in markets or online. Gently rub it on the affected areas.

REPTILE

File snake

ABORIGINAL NAME/S

kedjebe
Kunwinjku tribe, western Arnhem Land, NT

SCIENTIFIC NAME

Acrochordus arafurae

The file snake is a non-venomous water snake which is predominantly found in freshwater swamps, creeks and billabongs in Arnhem Land in the Northern Territory. You can identify a file snake quite easily as they are light–dark brown with a very thick body and a small, bulldog-shaped head. The females are larger than the males; they can grow as long as 2.5m and weigh about 1.5kg.

File snakes are called file snakes because of their rough, spiky, scaly, file-texture skin. They mostly breed in the dry season and the females only breed once every few years giving birth to approximately 20–30 babies, if the eggs survive attacks from crocodiles and birds.

They are also known as elephant trunk snake, Arafura file snake or wrinkle file snake.

TRADITIONAL USE

In the far north Arnhem Land region the Aboriginal women and children often hunt for file snakes, as they are a common bush tukka and are easy to find because these docile water snakes rest in the mud, in slow water or even on the banks of rivers. The women and children walk through crocodile-infested waters using their feet to feel around in the mud; when they feel something scaly, they reach down and grab the file snake and reach for its head to kill it instantly. They cook it whole on hot coals for 15–20 minutes. The flesh is white. It has a sweet flavour and a stringy texture; it's very similar to chicken but file snake has fattier flesh.

Yolŋu People in north-east Arnhem Land have a spiritual connection to the file snake, not only as a food source, but also as an ancient totemic symbol. It features heavily in their artwork and stories as the rainbow serpent and lightning spirit: creator of the waterholes, rivers, hills, valleys and mountains as it moved across the land.

OTHER USES

File snakes aren't used in a commercial sense, as it's more of a traditional food. People still find it hard to gather the courage to eat snake as it's far from being fish or chicken. But file snake has high levels of protein and omega oils and is a clean, fresh meat to eat.

FISH

Freshwater catfish

ABORIGINAL NAME/S

marrngunj
Kunwinjku tribe, western Arnhem Land, NT

SCIENTIFIC NAME

Neoarius leptaspis (boofhead catfish)

Catfish is one of those fish that is not taken seriously. They are bottom feeders and dwell in still water, generally out of the current of the main channels. Its colour varies between grey or golden brown, depending on size and water environment.

They grow to about 40–90cm in length. Catfish don't have scales, instead they have tough, leathery, sandpaper-like skin, which can make them difficult to handle. There is an important thing to know about catfish: they have sharp-edged spines in the dorsal and pectoral fins, which can penetrate the skin and inflict severe pain.

FISH

TRADITIONAL USE

Indigenous people cook catfish raised slightly above the hot coals; not having scales to protect its flesh, it is best to cook it above the heat to retain the natural oils and keep the flesh moist.

Most people turn their noses up at catfish, but Indigenous people really enjoy eating it, as it is fleshy and quite tasty.

Growing up in my community, every second house had a catfish crucifix. When a catfish was caught and eaten, someone would dry the skeleton out and either paint it or polish it to be used as a crucifix as the skeleton looks just like Jesus on the cross. I believe this is also practiced by other cultures around the world.

OTHER USES

Freshwater catfish flesh works well battered or grilled or in curries, stir-fries, fish stews and chowder.

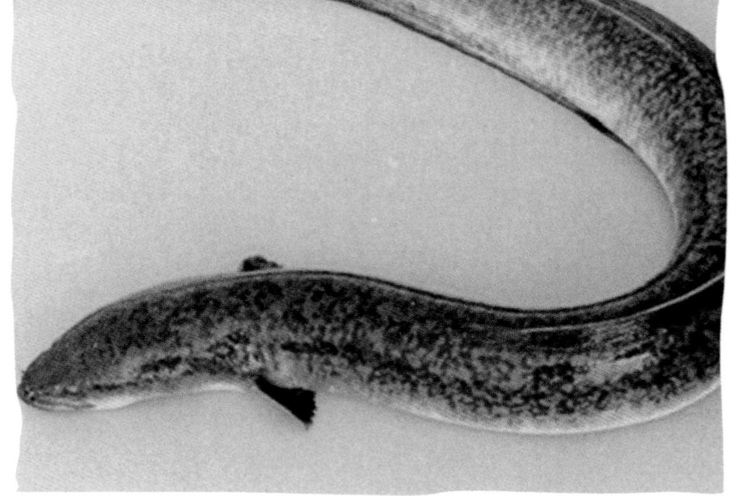

Freshwater eel

ABORIGINAL NAME/S

nyinggarra
Djabugay tribe, Kuranda, Far North Queensland

SCIENTIFIC NAME

Anguilla reinhardtii (Australian long-finned eel)

Freshwater eels are long and muscular, with brown–yellow skin when young, which eventually becomes mottled (for long-finned eels) or a dark olive colour (for short-finned eels) as they mature. They are diadromous, which means that they migrate between the sea and fresh water, mainly for breeding purposes. Their natural habitats are rivers, lakes, estuaries and creek systems. They make the big journey into the ocean to spawn.

Long-finned eels are a more tropical species, while short-finned eels like to live in milder waters, although both can be found up and down the east coast of Australia including South Australia, Tasmania, and as far as the Bass Strait Islands, Lord Howe Island, New Zealand and New Caledonia. They are well-travelled fish.

Freshwater eels are generally long and slimy, with snake-shaped bodies and small head. They usually have small pectoral fins to help them navigate along the river floor. They also have tiny, sandpapery teeth, so be careful when handling them.

TRADITIONAL USE

At Lake Condah in western Victoria, the Gunditjmara and the Djab Wurrung tribes were not nomads. Instead, they lived in permanent structures (stone dwellings) where they farmed eels in channels and ponds, formed by lava flows cutting deep channels in Country millennia ago. Evidence shows that in the 1800s Europeans moved in and drained the swampland but could not dismantle the natural channels created millions of years ago.

The Gunditjmara and the Djab Warrung People traded smoked eels with distant communities for other resources such as tools, weaponry and other foods. They used sophisticated methods of trapping eels by building long eel traps with holes at both ends to allow the eels to swim into the nets and then exit the end one by one, where they were collected and killed and put in eel-proof baskets. The eels were slow cooked above hot coals, or smoked in a blackwood tree and the oil was taken and rubbed over aching bones or limbs, or drunk for medicinal purposes.

OTHER USES

Eel is a delicacy all around the world and is farmed and cooked on a large scale commercially. The skin is quite oily and fatty but the flesh is slightly pink, turning white when cooked. It has a very firm texture and a distinctive rich, fleshy flavour. Eels are high in omega oils and protein, offering vitamins such as A, B1, B2 and E.

Because it has a high oil content, it's best to cook eel in ways that eliminate some of the oil, like poaching, steaming, grilling and smoking. Eel is great simmered in stews, but try not to serve eel raw because it does not have good raw texture.

If you can purchase eel from a fish market, it's best bought alive, but if not, you can get it with skin or skinless, filleted or as steaks.

SHELLFISH

Freshwater mud mussel

ABORIGINAL NAME/S

ngidjubany or gudjubay
Djabugay tribe, Kuranda, Far North Queensland

SCIENTIFIC NAME

Velesunio wilsonii

Freshwater mud mussels can be found in the muddy banks of brackish and fresh waters, mainly billabongs, rivers, creeks and lakes. Freshwater mussels prefer warmer climates.

Like common green mussels, freshwater mud mussels grow in black, ear-shaped shells. An adult mussel can grow up to 8–12cm long. The shell features radial markings, similar to tree-ring markings. It has a top and bottom that are joined by two very strong, white, sinew-like hinges. Inside, the shell is pearly white.

It holds a soft, rubbery, muscular, compact mussel, which is said to be not as tasty as its saltwater relative. These mussels are also filter feeders and are very sensitive to pollution.

TRADITIONAL USE

Freshwater mussels were traditionally an important source of food for Aboriginal People. Middens containing large numbers of mussel shells are widespread alongside rivers and lakes. Women and young girls would search for freshwater mud mussels while the men watched for crocodiles. The women and girls would immerse themselves in the water of creeks or rivers and swim along the banks, using their hands to dig around the muddy banks until they found a hard sharp object, which they would then dig out. They would fill their dilly bags, coolamons or paperbark baskets with the mussels.

The flesh was eaten after roasting in hot coals or boiling in water. Freshwater mud mussels were one of the foods Aboriginal People ate when they were in mourning.

The shell of a freshwater mud mussel has a pretty, lustrous sheen and is sometimes called pearl-shell. The mussel shells were also used as tools for carving or cutting.

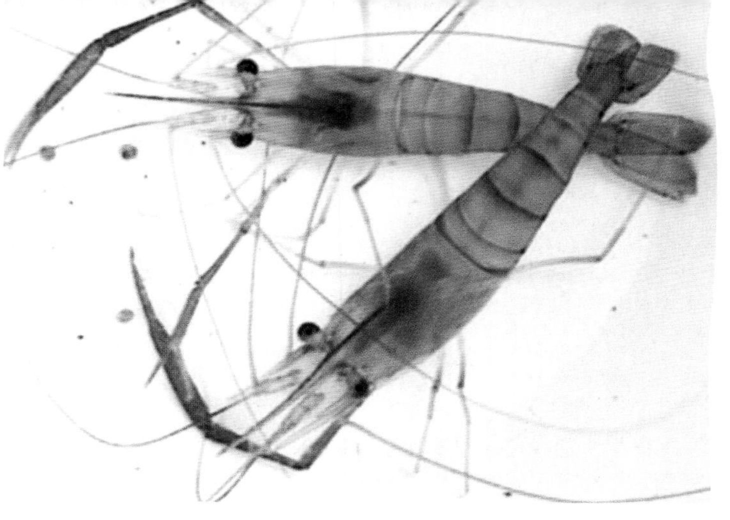

SHELLFISH

Freshwater prawn

ABORIGINAL NAME/S

Mindangmindang
Jawi tribe, West Kimberley, WA

SCIENTIFIC NAME

Macrobrachium species

Freshwater prawns (also known as cherabin, giant freshwater prawns, freshwater shrimps and inland crustaceans) are found in flowing or still waters such as rivers, creeks and billabongs, around rock ledges, under leaves and in hollow logs. They live in the warm waters throughout the northern regions of Australia, where they are called cherabin by the local Aboriginal communities throughout the Kimberley, Arnhem Land, Cape York and Gulf country. Cherabins are related to prawns and crayfish. They look very similar to prawns and crayfish, except that they have long, slender nippers, which are bright blue.

Cherabins can grow up to 15–30cm long and their body colour in the water is green and blue, allowing them to be camouflaged in freshwater environments. Their flesh is clear, almost transparent, but when cooked it turns white and their shells turn bright orange. The texture of the meat is similar to crayfish, but freshwater prawns are not as tasty as saltwater shellfish.

TRADITIONAL USE

The people in the Kimberley and Gulf country regard cherabin as a delicacy, and take pride in the hunting and gathering of it. The wet season floods are crucial for the survival of cherabins, particularly for breeding. Traditionally, before modern hunting tools were introduced, Aboriginal People would gather sticks and entwine them with a bit of string; they would tuck the bait tightly in the sticks so when the cherabin swims in to get the bait, it is difficult for it to come back out because the sticks would trap it. The women and children would also sit in the water dangling red meat around their bodies and when the cherabin would come to eat the bait, they would quickly grab them with their hands.

Cherabin can be eaten by roasting them in hot ashes. They can also be used as bait when fishing, however, most people think they are too valuable to be used as bait.

OTHER USES

Nowadays cast nets, freshwater pots and dilly pots (netted traps) seem to be the easiest way to catch cherabin. If using cast nets, spread or sprinkle chicken pellets in the water close to the bank and wait a few minutes before casting the nets. If using freshwater pots, people go crazy using all sorts of bait in the pots, from semi-boiled potatoes, tuna cans, soap bars, blocks of cheese and so on; when choosing your bait, please be mindful of what your bait is doing to the environment and how it could affect the other fish life in the water.

Cherabin are best cooked whole (shell and all) on the hot coals, to maintain the flavours. Some people like to cook them in stir-fries with Asian flavours, or simply barbecue or even boil them. Cherabin are just starting to appear on restaurant menus, mainly advertised as a bush tukka cuisine.

NOTE: For future generations, we encourage sustainable hunting and gathering practices and ask that you are mindful not to take more than you need, don't over fish the waterways and adhere to the limits in your state or territory, and don't take the female cherabin that is carrying eggs – be sure to place her back into the water immediately.

REPTILE

Goanna

ABORIGINAL NAME/S

barni
Bardi tribe, West Kimberley, WA

ganyal
Djabugay tribe, Kuranda, Far North Queensland

SCIENTIFIC NAME

Varanus

There are 30 species of goannas in the world and 25 of them are found in Australia. Goannas (otherwise called Australian monitors) are giant, carnivorous lizards with sharp teeth and claws. They can grow as big as 2–3m long, and prey on birds, bird eggs and smaller mammals. Goannas are mostly dark in colouring with camouflage tones of cream, grey, black, brown and green.

Goannas are land animals and are found all over Australia, mostly in warmer climates. They reside underground, in ground burrows or hollow logs, but with their sharp claws goannas can also climb tall trees to get away from predators and to hunt for baby birds or eggs in nests.

REPTILE

TRADITIONAL USE

Goannas are a delicacy amongst Aboriginal People. They feature strongly in Dreaming stories and as individual, family and clan spiritual totems. People who have an animal as a spiritual totem are responsible for the protection of that animal so it doesn't get over-hunted, and the spiritual stories attached to it are maintained. To dishonour a totemic animal can bring bad luck and bad energy to yourself, your family, your tribe or your land.

To hunt a goanna takes a lot of skill and energy; it involves tracking the goanna to find its burrow and then flushing it out to catch it. Goannas are extremely quick and if you miss it on the way out, you would have to be a very fast runner to chase it down. Most of the time, they run for the nearest tree, hollow log or burrow. If it climbs up a tree the only way to get it down is to stone it down, and if it runs into a hollow log the only way to get it out is to smoke it out by making a fire at one end to force the goanna out through the other end and have someone waiting to catch and kill it.

Aboriginal People cook goanna on hot coals: they make a fire and throw the goanna on the flames to burn off the tough layer of its skin; they let the fire burn down to coals then dig a hole in the middle of the hot coals, place the goanna inside and cover it with the hot coals for 30–40 minutes. The best parts of the goanna to eat are the legs and the tail. Goanna meat is white, and tastes like chicken breast, but a little drier. It is best eaten with the fat; this takes the experience to a whole other level, giving the meat the moisture and richness of the minerals in the fat. In western society eating fat is looked upon as unhealthy, but Aboriginal People eat everything; nothing goes to waste, and the fat is regarded as the prize of the animal because they believe it gives you energy and important natural minerals.

OTHER USES

Goanna oil was, and still is, an important bush medicine within Aboriginal communities. Its healing properties were used to rub on the skin as a natural moisturiser and to treat aching muscles and joints.

INSECT

Grasshopper

ABORIGINAL NAME/S

muurruung
Wiradjuri tribe, central NSW

SCIENTIFIC NAME

Orthoptera Caelifera

Grasshoppers can be found all over the world. They are interesting-looking insects with two big hind legs for jumping, and each leg has sharp defensive spikes on them. They have two pairs of narrow, transparent wings. They also have short antennae, prominent eyes, and two front and middle legs for balance.

Grasshoppers come out mainly in spring and summer, but they are most noticeable in autumn, when the large grasshoppers gather in groups, or swarms, causing plagues.

TRADITIONAL USE

Aboriginal People will eat grasshoppers by placing them on hot coals to crisp up. Just after the wet season, grasshoppers are like a plague and when there are so many of them, it makes them easy to catch.

Traditionally, women and children would have fun catching them. They would break off the legs so the grasshoppers could not hop away and then place them on the hot coals. Cooked this way, grasshoppers are crunchy, with a nutty flavour and full of protein.

They also make great bait when fishing for barramundi.

OTHER USES

A more contemporary way of cooking grasshopper is to collect 5–10 large grasshoppers, remove the legs and stir-fry them in hot oil with garlic and light soy sauce. They are really very tasty!

INSECT

Green ant

ABORIGINAL NAME/S

djiliburay
Djabugay tribe, Kuranda, Far North Queensland

SCIENTIFIC NAME

Oecophylla smaragdina

Green ants (also known as weaver ants) are found throughout northern Australia and south-east Queensland, in the open woodland and rainforests. They are called green ants because they have green abdomens. Green ants crawl over everything, but can be seen in trees, building their nest by weaving and gluing leaves together.

These extremely aggressive ants pack a punch if you're bitten, but they will only bite if they feel threatened or scared. Their little bodies are yellow, and they have six thin legs and two antennae, which are as long as their middle and back legs.

TRADITIONAL USE

Aboriginal People swear by the medicinal properties of green ants, offering dozes of vitamins and minerals. You can eat the ants individually by picking one up between your fingertips and biting off the green abdomen, then releasing the ant, giving you a tangy, mint flavour. The green abdomen acts as an antiviral agent for stomach aches and sore throats and other cold and flu symptoms. The ants can be squished between your hands and inhaled to clear the sinuses - the trick is to not get bitten.

To get a more potent effect, find a nest and boil it in hot water. Once you have boiled it for 10 minutes, let the liquid cool down and then place a clean cloth over the bowl and pour the liquid into another bowl, catching the ants in the cloth. Then wrap the cloth up and squeeze the remaining juice out of the ants. Aboriginal People use the liquid to treat sore throats, aching bones and headaches by pouring it over their heads or drinking it like a tea, warm or cool. They also add honey to sweeten it as the mixture has a tangy, bitter flavour.

OTHER USES

Green ants are the most valued insect eaten by humans because of their nutritional value. The ants are looked upon as a delicacy in countries like Thailand and Indonesia and are very expensive to buy.

INSECT

Honey ant

ABORIGINAL NAME/S

agkwarle yerrampe/ tjupi/tjala
Arrernte, Luritja and Pitjantjatjara tribes, central Australia, NT

SCIENTIFIC NAME

Camponotus inflatus

Honey ants are predominantly found in the hot, dry, arid terrains of the Western Desert regions of Australia. They live deep underground. Trapped by their pea-sized abdomen, which is filled with honey, they are unable to reach the surface, but they serve as living larders for other ants. While honeybees collect and store their liquids in a nest or in a comb, honey ants are unique as they store the liquid in their own bodies. They start off looking like normal ants. Worker

INSECT

ants feed them and they store the honey in their abdomens, which then grow into honeypots.

A honey ant has a little red head, black body and six little legs; the honey pot is round and golden with two thick black bands on the back.

TRADITIONAL USE

Aboriginal People from central Australia call honey ants ngkwarle yerrampe, which means 'honey ant Dreaming'. Aboriginal women will look for a small hole on the ground, which indicates the entrance of the nest below. They then dig into the ant colony to find the nest. They have to be gentle and patient because sometimes the nests are buried deep in the ground. Once they find the nest, they carefully pluck the honey ants out to collect and distribute them among the other women and children. They only eat the back of the ant, the honeypot, and then they place the ant back in the nest to reproduce. It's hard work, but when you find the honey ants it makes it all the more rewarding.

Honey ants also play an important part in the Dreaming stories of the Warlpiri People.

OTHER USES

Mostly honey ants are used as a sweet little treat, but the honey is also good for sore throats and is used for medicinal purposes as the honey is nutritious and contains antioxidants and has antiviral properties. It is also a good source of energy.

MAMMAL

Kangaroo

ABORIGINAL NAME/S

gangurru
Guugu Yimithir tribe, Far North Queensland

SCIENTIFIC NAME

Macropus rufus (red kangaroo), *Macropus giganteus* (eastern grey kangaroo), *Macropus fuliginosus* (western grey kangaroo), *Macropus antilopinus* (antilopine kangaroo)

The kangaroo is a marsupial with large powerful hind legs, large feet for leaping and a long muscular tail for balance. Different species of kangaroo can be found all over Australia. Like most marsupials, female kangaroos have a pouch where joeys (baby kangaroos) complete their postnatal development; a joey can stay in its mother's pouch for up to 18 months. Kangaroo fur is well designed for the Australian climate, being water-, heat- and cold-proof. They have incredible long ears to be able to hear from great distances, as well as great smell sense to sniff out danger. They also have extremely long eyelashes and a very small mouth with perfect grass-eating teeth.

Kangaroos don't live in any particular habitat. They are comfortable hopping all over the countryside, looking for food and water. They can reach hopping speeds of up to 70km per hour for nearly 2kms. But kangaroos are nocturnal animals, so when they need to rest during the day, they will find a nice shady tree to sleep under with a landscape where they can graze on grass during the night.

There are four different species of kangaroo. The red kangaroo is the largest and is found mostly in the arid and semi-arid centre of Australia. A male can grow as tall as 2m, and weigh 90–100kg. The eastern grey kangaroo is mostly found on the east coast of Australia. The western grey kangaroo is found across the southern part of Australia. The male is small, weighing approximately 54kg as an adult. The last one is the antilopine kangaroo, which lives in the far northern parts of Australia, enjoying the grassy plains and woodlands.

TRADITIONAL USE

The word kangaroo originated from the Guugu Yimithir word gangurru and was recorded in a diary entry by Sir Joseph Banks as kanguru.

Kangaroos play an important part in the Dreaming stories of many Aboriginal language groups across Australia, and it has spiritual totemic significance for some tribes.

Aboriginal men traditionally were the hunters of larger animals, especially kangaroo. They used weapons like the spear and woomera (a device which assisted the spear to be thrown faster, harder, more accurately and over longer distances). As with most bush tukka, every part of the kangaroo was used; nothing went to waste from the meat, to the fur, and even the sinew, which was used to bind weapons and tools. Once the animal was killed the kangaroo's warm blood would also be drained and shared amongst the men and boys of the tribe so that they could take on the strength, the speed and the wisdom of the animal.

OTHER USES

Kangaroo meat is believed to be the leanest meat on the market. High in protein, low in fat and rich in iron, kangaroo meat is full of flavour. It should be cooked medium–rare, on a sizzling hotplate or barbecue, to retain its natural juices and flavour. Kangaroo meat works extremely well in all dishes and styles of cooking from stir-fries, slow-cooked stews, curries and casseroles to kebabs, spaghetti sauce and roasts.

Kangaroo meat has become a commercial favourite; more and more restaurants are serving wonderful gourmet-style kangaroo dishes, but unfortunately people still have a reluctance to eat Skippy, from the well-loved Australian kids' television series *Skippy, the Bush Kangaroo*.

Magpie goose

ABORIGINAL NAME/S

djawadjawa dagi
Djabugay tribe, Kuranda, Far North Queensland

SCIENTIFIC NAME

Anseranas semipalmata

Magpie geese are large waterbirds that live mostly around savannah and northern coastal parts of Australia, like the Kimberley regions in Western Australia, the Top End in the Northern Territory, and in Far North Queensland. A magpie goose is black from the top of its head to the base of its neck, and has black wings. Its body is covered in white feathers, with orange legs and beak.

These classic birds can be found around wetlands, swamps, floodplains and cane paddocks, but they move around to different locations quite regularly during the dry season. They are also very noisy as they make a deep honking sound as a form of communication to others.

TRADITIONAL USE

The Ganalbingu, or Magpie Goose People, are the largest clan in central Arnhem Land. They have a respect for magpie geese and their spirit, as the magpie goose is part of the Ganalbingu Dreaming. Magpie goose eggs and nests are sacred as they are seen as the resting place for the geese's souls.

Aboriginal People of north central Arnhem Land cook magpie geese in a Bundatharri or Yathalamara: they make a fire on the hot coals, then they put paperbark leaves down and put the magpie geese on the leaves and then cover it with paperbark and sand until no steam is coming out; after 40 minutes they dust off the sand and remove the paperbark sheets to reveal steam-baked magpie geese.

OTHER USES

People in Arnhem Land still hunt and eat magpie geese today and prefer to prepare and cook it in the traditional ways. Magpie geese have dark, rich flesh, very similar to bustard meat but much more tender. Magpie geese have not reached the commercial food market, but the Aboriginal People of Arnhem Land treasure them.

MOLLUSC

Mangrove snail

ABORIGINAL NAME/S

djidin or gudjubay
Djabugay tribe, Kuranda, Far North Queensland

SCIENTIFIC NAME

Nerita lineata

Mangrove snails range in size from 1–2 cm at maturity. They can be found around rocky shores, reef rocks and mangrove vegetation, mostly in the northern regions of Australia. They are often found in large numbers, clustering together, near watermarks around mangrove roots.

The shell is rounded and durable, usually black or grey, with distinguishing black stripes down the back; underneath it is smooth, with a tinge of yellow at the outer entrance of the shell. The snail is pale with thin black bands on its single foot, and long, thin, black tentacles which act as sensors to help it become aware of predators like birds, crabs or humans. When the snails sense danger, they retreat into their shells. Mangrove snails have a little door or lid that seals off the snail inside the shell to protect it against predators.

Mangrove snails are herbivores. They feed on algae growing on reef rocks and mangrove roots.

You can use mangrove snails for bait. They are particularly good bait for barramundi.

TRADITIONAL USE

Aboriginal People in the far north Northern Territory and Far North Queensland (such as the Bama People) enjoy collecting mangrove snails (also known as periwinkles). They are best cooked on hot coals for 3–5 minutes, until you can see liquid bubbling from the entrance and when the lid begins to pop open. To access the snail, either crack the back of the shell or find a thin, sharp stick (like a toothpick or a needle) and peel the lid away, fishing out the snail at the same time. They can also be boiled in water for about 10 minutes.

OTHER USES

Mangrove snails have not really hit the commercial food industry, but they offer the same delicacy as land snails, or escargot, that are served as cherished appetisers in France. Cooked in the same manner as escargot (fried or baked in garlic herb butter) gives these miniature morsels a delightful twist of decadence.

Mangrove worm

ABORIGINAL NAME/S

latjin
Galiwin'ku tribe, Elcho Island, NT

SCIENTIFIC NAME

Teredo navalis

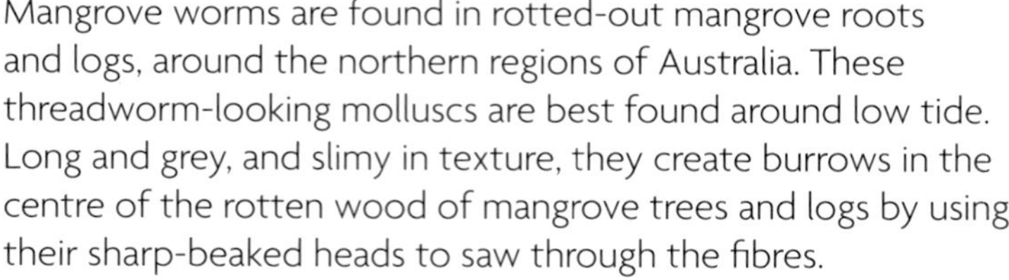

Mangrove worms are found in rotted-out mangrove roots and logs, around the northern regions of Australia. These threadworm-looking molluscs are best found around low tide. Long and grey, and slimy in texture, they create burrows in the centre of the rotten wood of mangrove trees and logs by using their sharp-beaked heads to saw through the fibres.

They like the coastal saltwater environments in warmer weather, and can grow as long as 40cm.

TRADITIONAL USE

Mangrove worms are highly regarded by the coastal Yolŋu People in far north Arnhem Land in the Northern Territory. The Yolŋu enjoy the worms, and are very good at tracking them and finding dead broken logs or dead roots where they can harvest mangrove worms nesting inside. Mangrove worms are mostly eaten raw.

OTHER USES

Mangrove worms are not the type of bush tukka you will find on the menu in a restaurant. They should be kept and eaten in their natural habitat, but in saying that, these slimy little morsels are a delicacy to Aboriginal People, and taste very similar to oysters. Mangrove worms are also a rich source of protein and iron.

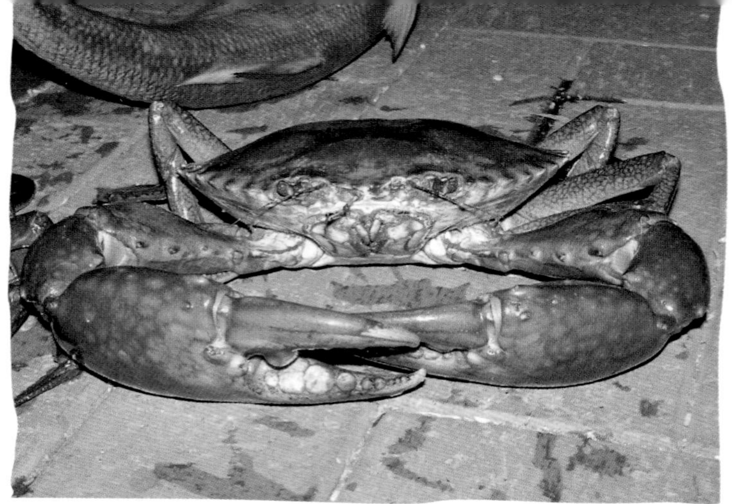

Mud crab

ABORIGINAL NAME/S

ngudoong
Jawi tribe, West Kimberley, WA

SCIENTIFIC NAME

Scylla serrata

Mud crabs are abundant in estuaries, mangrove swamps, creeks and rivers, and in more protected environments like under mangroves roots, in mud and water pools. Two species of mud crabs are found in Australia: green mud crabs and brown mud crabs. Throughout north-west Western Australia, the top of the Northern Territory, Queensland and New South Wales, recreational fishers can harvest mud crabs by hand (depending on locations within each state or territory), using traps, traditional spears, crab hooks, dilly pots and lift nets.

A mature green mud crab can grow up to 30cm wide, and weigh 2.5kg. The brown mud crab grows to half the size of a green mud crab: 15cm wide, and weighs 1.5kg.

Female crabs are protected; if you catch a jenny crab (as a female crab is called) you must release it back into the mud or water. You can easily tell a jenny crab by its abdominal flaps, which are much broader than the male or 'buck' abdominal flaps. Also, when jenny crabs reach their mature cycle, their claws are a lot smaller than a male crab. Do your research before you go mud crabbing to avoid heavy fines if you're caught with jenny crabs.

When catching mud crab by hand, be very careful as their nippers can cut through almost anything and can certainly take off your fingers. It is best to approach a mud crab from behind and hold its body down using a stick and then grab the back swimmer-legs in a firm lock. The nippers will rise to try to attack you, but they don't go backwards so you can catch it this way without getting hurt.

TRADITIONAL USE

Aboriginal People have enjoyed mud crab hunting for thousands of years. The first sign of when mud crabs are ready to be hunted is when the bark on the eucalypts starts to peel away from the tree. Although the method of hunting for mud crabs has advanced somewhat, it is still a lot of fun for the whole family!

Aboriginal People used to catch mud crabs by hand or using a stick or spears to force them from their burrows. Hunting this way takes a lot of energy: walking through the thick, wet mud of sandfly- and mosquito-infested mangroves, and climbing over the entwined mangrove roots. It was and is hard work, so they only took the respectful amount needed to feed their families as they were aware they still had to carry the heavy mud crabs back the way they had come.

The traditional way to cook mud crabs is on hot coals. Some people may think this is cruel, but this has been a cooking method for thousands of years. Cooking foods directly on the coals is a much healthier way to cook because it maintains the nutrients of the food which can be lost through other cooking methods.

Every part of the mud crab is eaten. The best part is what Indigenous people call 'the soup'. This is the guts of the crab: the yellow and white creamy substance you find under the main shell when you peel it open. This creamy substance is rich in protein, vitamins and minerals including zinc and iron. The claws are also very yummy to eat because they have a different texture to the rest of the body, and nothing is wasted except the gills in the body, which are grey in colour and look like sharp fingers.

OTHER USES

Mud crabs can be cooked in so many ways. One of the most popular dishes is chilli mud crabs which traditionally originates from Singapore. Aboriginal People did not have chillies or sauces, this was introduced by the pearl drivers who ventured over from Singapore, Malaysia and Japan in the early 1970's. But earlier, in the 1700's there was evidence of tradings from the Macassan People of Indonesia to the Yolŋu People of Northern Arnhem Land, this is predating early European colonisation.

You can experiment using mud crabs in curries, stir-fries and even making crab cakes.

MOLLUSC

Mud whelk

ABORIGINAL NAME/S

damitjarra
Larrakia tribe, NT

SCIENTIFIC NAME

Telescopium telescopium

Mud whelks (also known as long bums) prefer the warm climates of Northern Australia, and can be found at low tide, living in muddy banks around mangrove vegetation and roots, and near watermarks. They are often found clustering together in large numbers. They have long, cone-shaped shells, which are brown with a creamy spiral pattern. The shells have a large opening at the wide end of the cone and can grow up to 11cm long.

Mud whelks belong to the same class of molluscs as the mangrove snails but mud whelks have a more conical shell.

These shells, sometimes house hermit crabs, so you must be careful when gathering and cooking them. You can tell that a mud whelk lives inside the shell by the colour of the inside shell which should be light blue. The mud whelk itself is the most amazing bright blue colour that you will ever see in a snail.

When collecting mud whelks, you're best to take a bucket, as they are quite large in size. When you cook mud whelks on the hot coals, it's best to place them sharp end down with the open end sticking out of the coals; this way the whole snail will cook thoroughly.

To get the snail out of the shell you need to poke it with a sharp metal object. But there is a trick to it, as the snail will break if you're not careful and gentle in pulling it out. Another way is to get a hard object and break the side of the shell after it has been cooked (when it is easier to break open); then you can fish out the snail, splitting the body in half.

TRADITIONAL USE

Mud whelks are a delicacy among Aboriginal People. Most Aboriginal People cook mud whelk shells on hot coals or boil them in hot water.

Aboriginal People eat mud whelks to fight viral and chest infections because of their rich mineral content.

OTHER USES

Mud whelks have not reached the commercial market as they are not seen as an attractive bush tukka, and are very hard to harvest. The taste of mud whelks is quite salty. They are a rich source of sodium, iron and protein. You should not eat too many however, because these snails can give you diarrhoea if eaten in large quantities.

SHELLFISH

Native milky oyster

ABORIGINAL NAME/S

bandin
Djabugay tribe, Kuranda, Far North Queensland

SCIENTIFIC NAME

Saccostrea cucullata

There are many species of oysters, but native milky oysters should not be confused with pearl oysters, which are not edible. Native milky oysters can be found growing in huddles or clusters on anything solid from mangrove roots to reef shelves to rocky walls. They prefer to live in sheltered surroundings where the surface water is warm enough for spawning in summer. They can also be found growing in most estuaries and bays along the northern, eastern and southern coasts of Australia. Some oysters grow up to 8–12cm in size and, if you're lucky, you can find oysters the size of a dinner plate!

Native milky oysters grow in an ear-shaped little cup or shell, with a lid, but they vary in size depending on the surface on which they grow, such as rocks, mangroves, wooden or concrete pylons, or around boat ramps and jetties. The shells are generally grey with jagged, waved edges around the lip of the lid, which is generally shut tight. Inside the shell, the oyster body is cream but the gills are black and grey, and the shell on the inside is white with a smooth, porcelain surface.

Native milky oysters are easy to harvest or collect off the rocks, but they are hard to collect without entirely destroying them. You can neatly scrape the oysters off the rocks with a screwdriver and a hammer. If you don't have these tools, then find a hard, longish rock with a pointy end to use as a hammer to crack the oysters open. Be careful not to crack the oysters directly on top and squash the lid onto it, but to tap them from the side; you will see how the lids start to open. Once you have loosened the lid, remove the oyster from its shell. This can be tricky because the oyster muscles are very strong. You can eat the oyster raw, straight from the shell, or try to crack the whole shell off the rocks and then cook it on hot coals.

TRADITIONAL USE

Native milky oysters are abundant bush tukka. With easy harvesting at low tide, collecting oysters is fun for Aboriginal women and children, and it does not take up a lot of energy. Oysters have been a staple food for coastal saltwater Aboriginal People for thousands of years.

OTHER USES

Native milky oysters are a huge commercial bush tukka and restaurants have many ways of serving them. Oysters in the western world are very expensive and highly prized.

Restaurants buy their oysters directly from oyster farms – that way they know they are getting healthy, good-quality oysters. Restaurants seek closed oysters. They shuck or open them freshly in their kitchens using special oyster knives and heavy-duty gloves to prevent any oyster cuts; that way the oysters are fresh.

The wonderful thing about oysters is that they can be eaten raw or cooked. There are many creative ways to cook oysters, but the most common ways are oysters kilpatrick or served with a cheesy mornay sauce.

Oysters have been proven to have high levels of zinc, calcium and iron, as well as vitamins A and B12, and studies have found them to be most nutritious when eaten raw.

Saltwater mud mussel

ABORIGINAL NAME/S

djulwa
Djabugay tribe, Kuranda, Far North Queensland

SCIENTIFIC NAME

Polymesoda coaxans

Saltwater mud mussels prefer saltwater mud and mangrove environments; they like warm, dry climates and can be found at low tide, predominantly around the north-western and north-eastern parts of Australia. The length of a mature mud mussel is 8–12cm. The shell features radial markings, similar to tree-ring markings. Mud mussels range in colour from black at the tip of the shell to brown and white around the base of the shell. Inside, the mussel is quite fleshy, but it decreases to the size of a 20-cent piece when cooked.

To find saltwater mud mussels, look for evidence of large, black shells in the mud, or small holes on the surface of the mud through which the mussels breathe. The mussels are usually embedded deep in mangrove mudflats, so you have to sit and dig in the mud with your hands to find them, if you're lucky you will find them on the surface of the mud as they make their way across the mud to find another home. You can also find mussels in dry, cracked mud: look out for a small straight opening, about 25mm long, slightly covered in the mud. They're not easy to find, but once you know what you're looking for, you will start to see the landscape differently.

TRADITIONAL USE

Saltwater mud mussels are a delicacy for the northern Arnhem Land Yolŋu People. They are a valued food source for Indigenous Saltwater People, providing high levels of protein, zinc, iron and vitamins. Although different tribes call them different names, the hunting and cooking techniques are pretty much the same. After a day of gathering the mussels in the mangroves, the Yolŋu People find a nice shady tree, light a fire and place the mussels on the hot coals. After about 5 minutes the shells start to open, indicating that the mussels are ready to eat.

Another way the Yolŋu People like to cook mud mussels is to boil them in hot water. This gives the mussels a rubbery texture, but a creamier taste. The Yolŋu People also drink the warm, salty water the mussels were cooked in to get the rich minerals from the mussels, which help the body fight colds and other viruses. They are a valued food source, providing high levels of protein, zinc, iron and vitamins.

INSECT

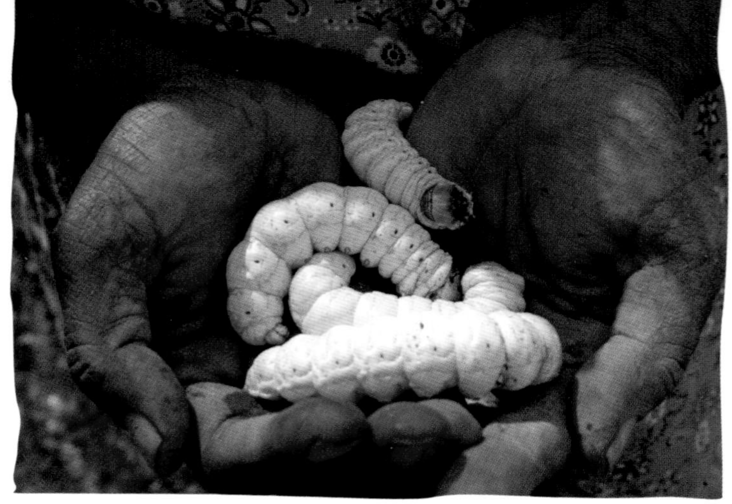

Witchetty grub

ABORIGINAL NAME/S

maku
Aṉangu tribe, central NT

SCIENTIFIC NAME

Endoxyla leucomochla

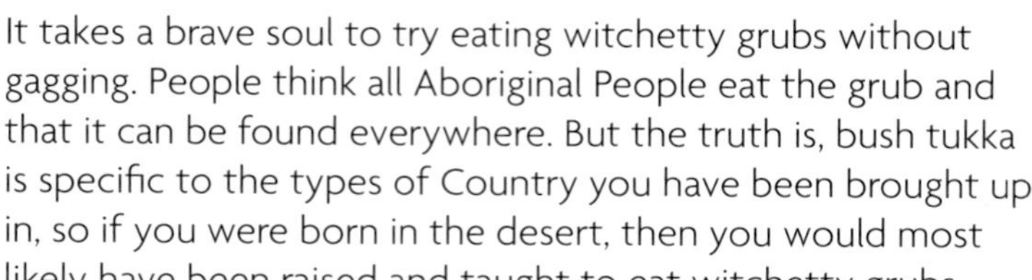

It takes a brave soul to try eating witchetty grubs without gagging. People think all Aboriginal People eat the grub and that it can be found everywhere. But the truth is, bush tukka is specific to the types of Country you have been brought up in, so if you were born in the desert, then you would most likely have been raised and taught to eat witchetty grubs.

Witchetty grubs are an all-time favourite bush tukka. They are the wood-eating larvae of a moth. They are found eating through the roots of river red gum, the wichetty bush, the small cooba and bloodwood trees in the central deserts of Australia.

Witchetty grubs are white with a yellow head and soft skin. They grow as fat as 1.5cm thick, and as long as 12cm.

TRADITIONAL USE

These grubs are a staple of the diets of Aboriginal People in the desert. Although it's hard work digging for the grubs, only the women dig for them. When they have collected enough, they light a small fire and throw the grubs onto the hot coals and cover them with hot ash to cook for about 5 minutes. The grubs have a nutty flavour, and a texture very similar to warm scrambled eggs, but if eaten raw the grubs are soft and slimy with a sweet flavour. It's best to eat the grubs whole, in one go.

OTHER USES

Witchetty grubs are a famous bush tukka that everyone refers to when bush tukka is mentioned. Commercial chefs use witchetty grubs to promote bush tukka in their restaurants. Everyone should try them at least once in their life. For the more squeamish stomachs, witchetty grubs are best eaten cooked, which is a simple process of lightly frying them in a frying pan, with or without oil, for approximately 5–10 minutes, turning continuously to allow them to cook evenly.

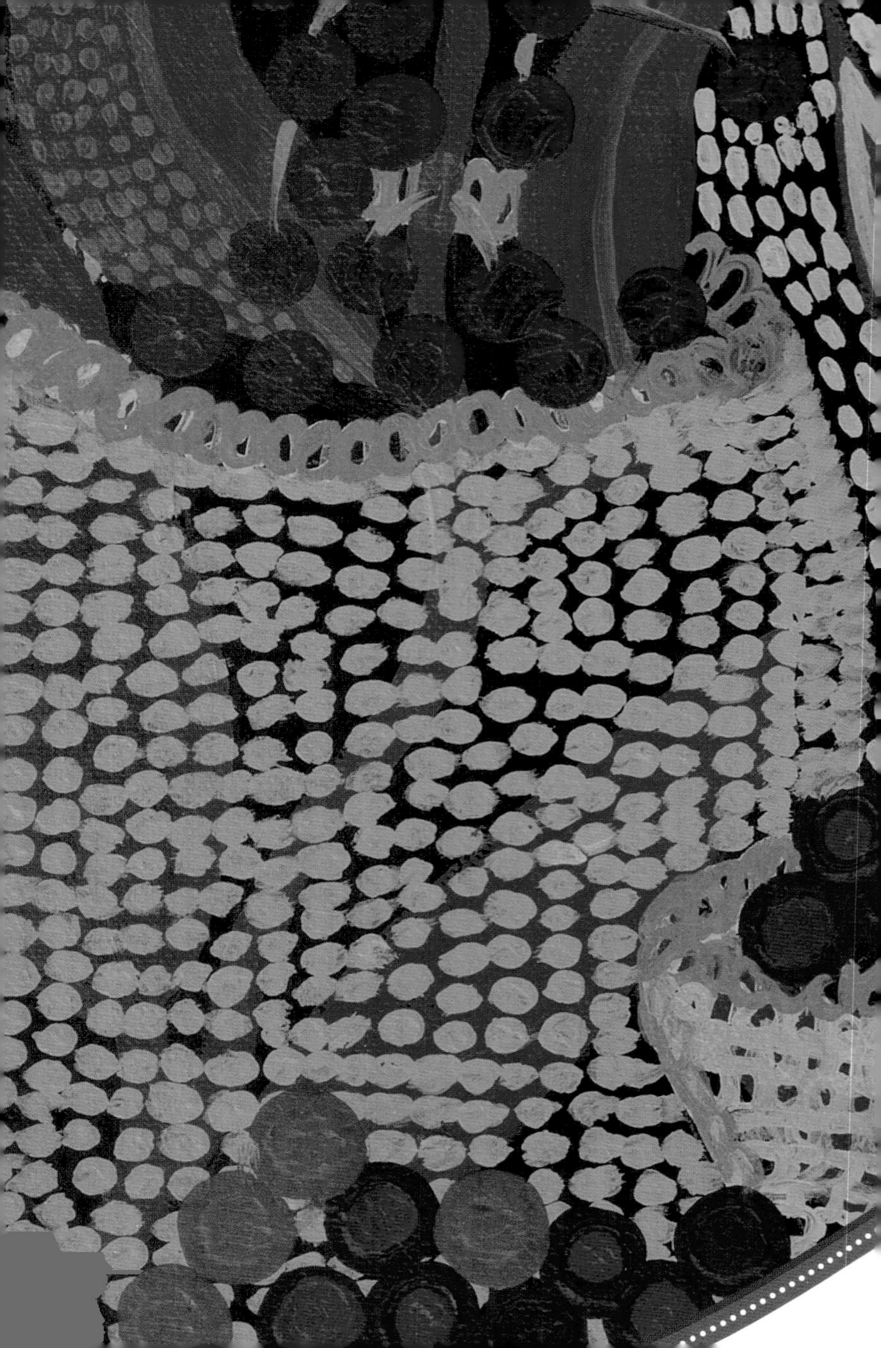

Recipes

Lemon myrtle rustic damper

65 min

Serves 10–12

INGREDIENTS

- 3 cups self-raising flour
- pinch of salt
- 80g butter, melted
- 30g finely ground lemon myrtle leaves
- ¾ cup warm water

Damper is highly celebrated in many Aboriginal and Torres Strait Islander communities, however, damper cooked today is very different to how it was cooked it in the past. Originally, they only used ground seeds, nuts and roots which were all unprocessed, this resulted in a much healthier product.

What I would like to highlight is that damper is among some of the worst foods Indigenous people could eat. White flour and white sugar have had a heavy impact on the health of Aboriginal and Torres Strait Islander people, many of whom are suffering with chronic diseases and health conditions. I urge you to avoid regularly consuming foods like this and to learn more about creating healthy and balanced diets.

METHOD

1. Preheat the oven to 200°C, and grease a large baking tray well with oil or butter.
2. Combine the flour, salt, butter and finely ground lemon myrtle leaves in a large mixing bowl and, using your fingers, rub all the ingredients together until it resembles a crumbly mixture.
3. Slowly add the water to the mixture and stir well with a large mixing spoon, until the mixture starts to blend together, adding small amounts of water if the mixture gets too dry.
4. Once the mixture becomes like dough, place onto a dry, well-floured surface and use your hands to knead it gently until firm (roughly 2–3 minutes). The dough should be smooth, not sticky.
5. Shape the dough into a disc and place it onto your baking tray. Take a sharp knife and make shallow cuts into the dough, like cutting a pizza, and sprinkle with flour.
6. Bake for 30–40 minutes, until golden brown and cooked through in the middle. Transfer to a wire rack and let cool for 5 minutes. Slice and spread with butter, jam or honey.

Native bush dukkah

5 min

Makes 200g

INGREDIENTS

- 25g dried bush tomatoes, whole or crushed
- 25g dried lemon myrtle leaves, whole leaves or crushed
- 10g wattleseed, whole or crushed
- 10g mountain bush pepper, whole or crushed
- 10g saltbush or sea salt, whole or crushed
- 100g roasted macadamias, whole or crushed

METHOD

1. If you are using whole ingredients, put the bush tomatoes, lemon myrtle leaves, wattleseeds, mountain bush pepper and saltbush/sea salt into a food processor or blender, and grind coarsely. Add the roasted macadamias, and grind a little more, until powdered to your liking.
2. If you are using crushed ingredients, put all the ingredients into a sealable sandwich bag and shake well. Crush the roasted macadamias and add to the mixture, combining all ingredients well.

Best served with Australian olive oil and damper or fresh rustic bread.

Bunya nut pesto

15 min

Makes 250g

INGREDIENTS

- 1 cup bunya nuts, cooked, peeled and shucked
- ½ bunch basil leaves
- ½ bunch rocket
- 4 garlic cloves
- 1 chilli
- 2 tablespoons lemon juice
- ¼ cup oil

Bunya nut preparation

1. Place bunya nuts in a pot of boiling water with a pinch of salt. Boil for half an hour, or until the water turns brown and you see the tip of the nuts open slightly.
2. To open or shuck a bunya nut, place a small knife at the tip, where it is slightly open, and cut ¾ into the shell. Once you have made a cut, you can then peel the shell off to reveal the nut inside.

METHOD

1. Shuck all bunya nuts and place in a food processor and process until slightly crushed. Add basil, rocket, garlic and chilli, and process until all ingredients are combined.
2. Add lemon juice and oil, and process a little more to mix through.

Serve with crusty bread or crackers. Or you can use the pesto in pasta, fish, chicken or pork dishes; this pesto is especially great for marinating chicken and seafood. You can also pour the pesto into a jar and use at your own leisure. It will keep in the refrigerator for up to 2–3 weeks.

Stir-fried grasshoppers

15 min

Serves 4

INGREDIENTS

- 4 tablespoons oil
- 1 teaspoon sesame oil
- 2 tablespoons light soy sauce
- 1 large brown onion, diced
- 4 garlic cloves, crushed
- 1 large red chilli, deseeded (optional)
- 2 shallots, sliced
- 10–15 large brown grasshoppers, legs removed

METHOD

1. Heat oil, sesame oil and soy sauce in a wok.
2. Add the onion, garlic, chilli and shallots, and fry until the onion is slightly transparent.
3. Add the grasshoppers and cook until they turn slightly brown.

Serve immediately.

NOTE: Grasshoppers will keep in the freezer for up to 6 weeks, so you can collect and store them until you have enough for a whole dish. Just make sure you fully thaw them before cooking.

Mangrove snails with garlic butter

20 min

Serves 6

INGREDIENTS

- 125g butter
- 1 onion, finely chopped
- 4 garlic cloves, finely chopped
- 2 lemon myrtle leaves (fresh or dried)
- ½ cup white wine
- 1 tablespoon brown sugar
- 1kg mangrove snails or periwinkles
- ½ cup fresh parsley, finely chopped

METHOD

1. Melt butter in a large pot. Add onion, garlic and lemon myrtle leaves to the melted butter, and cook until the onion becomes transparent.
2. Add the wine and sugar, and bring to the boil. Then add the mangrove snails or periwinkles and parsley. Stir well. Cover and simmer for 10 minutes.

Serve with crusty bread on a bed of rice or spaghetti.

Crocodile, ginger & vegetable stir-fry

40 min

Serves 4–6

INGREDIENTS

Marinade

- 2 tablespoons light soy sauce
- 1 teaspoon crushed ginger
- ¼ teaspoon salt
- 500g crocodile minya (meat), sliced

Stir fry

- 2 tablespoons oil (1 tablespoon if using a non-stick pan)
- 1 brown onion, sliced
- 1 tablespoon crushed ginger
- 3 garlic cloves, roughly chopped
- 4 tablespoons light soy
- 2 tablespoons dark soy

- 4 tablespoons sweet chilli sauce
- 4 tablespoons oyster sauce
- 2 tablespoons each-ground lemon myrtle, mountain pepper, saltbush and wattleseed
- 2 medium carrots, sliced
- ½ broccoli, chopped
- 1 red capsicum, cut into strips
- 400g can baby corn, drained
- 1 zucchini, sliced
- 8 button mushrooms
- 10 snow peas, sliced lengthways
- 2 tablespoons sesame seeds

METHOD

1. In a large bowl, combine the light soy, crushed ginger, salt and sliced crocodile. Mix well and leave to marinate for at least 30 minutes.
2. Set a large wok or frying pan over a medium–high heat and add oil. Add the onions, ginger and garlic, cook until the onion is translucent. Add the sauces (light soy, dark soy, sweet chilli, oyster sauce) and the ground herbs. Cook until bubbling.
3. Add your minya (meat) and cook thoroughly. Remove from the pan and set it aside.
4. Add vegetables: carrots first, then broccoli, capsicum, baby corn, zucchini, mushrooms and snow peas. Stirring until all cooked through.
5. Return the minya to the pan with the vegetables and mix well. Sprinkle over the sesame seeds.

Serve with rice or noodles.

Curried crocodile and potato mash

65 min

Serves 4

INGREDIENTS

Curried crocodile

- 2 tablespoons oil
- 1 large onion, diced
- 2 garlic cloves, crushed
- 1kg crocodile fillets, sliced
- 2 carrots, thinly sliced
- 2 sticks celery, thinly sliced
- 6 lemon myrtle leaves (fresh or dried)
- 2 tablespoons dry curry powder
- 400g can diced tomatoes
- 1 teaspoon brown sugar
- 1 tablespoon chicken stock
- ½ cup water

Potato mash

- 4 large potatoes, peeled and diced
- 1 tablespoon butter
- dash of milk
- pinch of salt

METHOD

Curried crocodile

1. Heat the oil in a pot. Once the oil is hot, fry the onion, garlic, crocodile, carrots, celery and lemon myrtle leaves until the onion softens and crocodile browns.
2. Add curry powder, tomatoes, brown sugar and chicken stock, and stir well, until ingredients are mixed together. Add water if the mixture is dry.
3. When crocodile is fully cooked through (it will be white in colour and firm to the touch), remove from the heat.

Potato mash

1. Boil diced potatoes until soft. Drain water, then add butter, milk and salt to potatoes and mash to your liking.

Serve the curried crocodile on top of the potato mash. Garnish with finely sliced shallots or parsley.

Chilli and bush tomato mud crabs

35 min

Serves 4

INGREDIENTS

Mud crabs

- 2 mud crabs
- 2 tablespoons olive oil
- 1 large onion, finely diced
- 4 garlic cloves, finely crushed
- 2 teaspoons ginger, finely crushed

Chilli sauce

- 400g can crushed tomatoes
- ½ cup sweet chilli sauce
- ½ cup tomato paste
- 2 tablespoons fish sauce
- 1 tablespoon palm sugar
- 2 lemon myrtle leaves (fresh or dried)
- 2 tablespoons crushed bush tomatoes
- 1 tablespoon white vinegar
- 5 fresh basil leaves, finely sliced

METHOD

Mud crabs

1. To prepare the mud crabs, lift the top of the crab shell from the rest of the body, then remove and discard the long, grey lungs. Rinse the crab well and cut it in half down the middle, and then in half again, separating the legs.
2. In a large wok, heat the oil. Add the onions, garlic and ginger. Toss until onion starts to brown.
3. Add crab quarters and toss until the crab turns a slight orange colour; remove from the wok and place to the side whilst you cook the sauce. Take care not to overcook the crab here as it will be returned to the pan to cook through in the sauce.

Chilli sauce

1. Add the tomatoes, chilli sauce, tomato paste, fish sauce, palm sugar, lemon myrtle leaves, bush tomatoes and white vinegar to the wok and stir well. Leave until the sauce starts to bubble, then return the mud crabs to the wok. Stir well and bring to the boil.
2. Cover and let simmer for 10 minutes, until all crab pieces turn bright orange.
3. Sprinkle with finely chopped basil for presentation.

Serve with rice or crusty bread.

Garlic cherabin stirfry

30 min

Serves 6

INGREDIENTS

- 500g fresh cherabin (freshwater prawns)
- 2 tablespoons oil
- 50g butter
- 1 large brown onion, diced
- 4 garlic cloves, crushed
- 1 large red chilli, deseeded (optional)
- 2 shallots, diced
- 2 tablespoons chicken stock

METHOD

1. Remove the heads and peel the shells off the cherabins, keeping the heads to include in the dish.
2. Add oil and butter to a frying pan on high heat. Once hot, add the onion, garlic, chilli and shallots, and fry until the onion is slightly transparent.
3. Add the cherabin and cook until they turn slightly orange in colour and the flesh is white and firm.

Serve on a bed of jasmine rice.

NOTE: this dish is best eaten fresh. Many people discard the heads when cooking cherabin or prawns, however they hold a lot of flavour that will enhance your dish should you choose to keep them in.

Baked barramundi in lemon myrtle butter

65 min

Serves 4

INGREDIENTS

- olive oil
- 4 barramundi fillets
- 100g butter
- 2 tablespoons, ground lemon myrtle leaves
- 8 fresh lemon myrtle leaves
- 2 tablespoons ground saltbush

METHOD

1. Preheat oven to 180°C. Lightly brush olive oil onto four sheets of aluminium foil and place a barramundi fillet onto each.
2. Bring butter to room temperature in a small mixing bowl. Stir the ground lemon myrtle and saltbush into the butter and mix until well combined.
3. Take a scoop of the butter mix and smear over the fish fillets. Top each fillet with 2 lemon myrtle leaves. Fold the edges of the foil over the fish, then wrap each one in a second sheet of foil to create a tightly sealed parcel.
4. Place on a tray in the oven and bake for 10–15 minutes. Turn the parcels over and bake for another 10–15 minutes.

Serve with a green salad, rice or baked potatoes.

Mountain bush pepper and lemon aspen whole-baked barramundi

55 min

Serves 2

INGREDIENTS

- 1 whole barramundi, scaled and gutted
- ½ teaspoon mountain bush pepper, crushed
- 4 tablespoons of light soy sauce
- 10 lemon aspens, sliced
- large knob of ginger, julienned
- 3 garlic cloves, crushed
- 1 red chilli, deseeded and thinly sliced
- 3 spring onions, thinly sliced
- 10 dried or fresh lemon myrtle leaves

METHOD

1. Preheat oven at 250°C for 20 minutes, then turn down to 180°C.
2. Rinse your barramundi and dry well. Make several cuts, about 2-3cm apart, into both sides of the barramundi. Rub mountain pepper and push folded lemon myrtle leaves into the cuts.
3. Lay a large sheet of baking paper on a tray and place the barramundi in the center. Pour soy sauce over the fish and place the thin slices of lemon aspen, ginger, garlic, red chilli and spring onions over the flesh.
4. Once the barramundi is dressed up, grab the corners of the baking paper and bring to the center. Fold over to create a parcel, ensuring you leave a little hole to allow for the steaming process.
5. Cook for 25–35 minutes. If your fish is larger, cook for 35–45 minutes or until the fish flesh turns white.

Serve on a bed of rice or with a salad of your choice.

Lemon myrtle pipis – two ways

75 min

Serves 4–6

The base of this recipe is a hearty stew, which, by adding cream, can be transformed into a rich chowder. I've included instructions for both, so you can simply let your tastebuds decide. If you're unable to gather fresh pipis, you can purchase them prepackaged in most supermarkets or seafood shops.

INGREDIENTS

Pipi stew

- 60–80g each butter and olive oil
- 4 lemon myrtle leaves, fresh or dried
- 2 rashers bacon, roughly chopped
- 1 onion, roughly chopped
- 2 garlic cloves, finely chopped
- 2 celery stalks, diced (include the leaves)
- 1 red capsicum, diced
- 2 carrots, diced

- 400g tin corn kernels
- 4 large potatoes, peeled and diced
- 2 litres chicken stock or water
- salt and pepper
- 1kg pipis (or whatever fresh seafood is available, such as mussels or fish)
- ½ cup white wine
- 1–2 teaspoons corn flour (optional)
- 1 cup flat-leaf parsley, roughly chopped

Pipi chowder (in addition to ingredients above)

- ½ cup thickened cream, depending on the pot size

METHOD

1. Clean and prepare the pipis (see page 106) and set aside.
2. Warm a heavy-base saucepan or pot to a medium-high heat and add the butter and oil. Scrunch up the lemon myrtle leaves and add to the pan along with the chopped bacon; cook until slightly crispy. Add the onions, garlic, celery, capsicum and carrot. Cook until the celery and vegetables are cooked through.
3. Add the corn kernels, potatoes and chicken stock. Bring to the boil and cook until tender. Season well with salt and pepper.
4. Add the pipis to the pot and stir in well, ensuring they are covered with liquid. Turn the heat off once the pipis open place aside ready for serving.

Serve with damper or crusty bread and add the parsley to garnish.

NOTE: For the chowder version – stir through the cream once the pipis are added and have started to open. Add corn flour to thicken if it's too runny and mix well.

Lemon myrtle-crusted fish tacos

50 min

Serves 6

INGREDIENTS

Cabbage slaw

- 3 cups green and purple cabbage, finely shredded
- ½ cup red onion, diced
- 1 cup sour cream (plus extra for serving)
- 1 lime, juiced
- ¼ teaspoon salt

Salsa

- ½ cup corn kernels, fresh cut off the cob or canned
- 1 red onion, diced
- 1 punnet cherry tomatoes, diced
- 1 bunch coriander, roughly chopped
- 2 garlic cloves, crushed
- 2 avocados, diced
- 1 lime
- salt and lemon myrtle, to taste

Tacos

- 4 fish fillets (Mackerel, snapper or any fish you prefer)
- potato flour or any flour to coat the protein
- 1 tablespoon each- ground lemon myrtle, mountain pepper, saltbush and wattleseed
- ¼ teaspoon garlic powder
- ¼ teaspoon cumin
- ¼ teaspoon salt
- ¼ teaspoon pepper
- 12 corn tortillas
- coriander
- 1 lime, cut into wedges

METHOD

1. In a large bowl, combine all the cabbage slaw ingredients and mix until well coated. Chill until ready to serve.
2. In a separate bowl, combine the salsa ingredients, drizzle with lime juice and a pinch of salt and lemon myrtle.
3. In another bowl, mix the mountain pepper, saltbush, wattleseed, garlic powder, cumin, salt and pepper. Coat the fish fillets in the potato flour then toss in the spice mix. Be sure to coat both sides of each fillet.
4. In a frying pan over medium–high heat, cook the fillets for approximately 8 minutes (or until cooked), flipping halfway.
5. Before serving, heat the corn tortillas in a pan over high heat. Remove from the pan and assemble the tacos with the cabbage slaw and fish.
6. Garnish with the coriander, lime juice, sour cream and salsa.

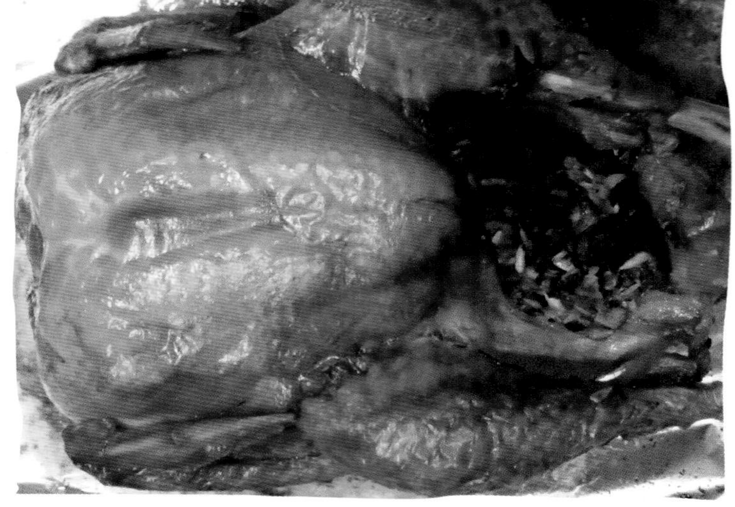

Camp oven-roasted bustard bird and vegetables

70 min

Serves 8–10

INGREDIENTS

- 1 bustard bird
- oil
- salt and pepper
- 6–10 lemon myrtle leaves, fresh or dried
- 2 carrots, grated
- 6 garlic cloves, crushed
- 3 onions, finely diced
- 3 celery sticks, finely diced

METHOD

1. First, prepare the fire with hot coals and make sure the camp oven is well oiled. Then pluck the bustard and remove the guts.
2. Smear oil all over the bird and season well with salt, pepper and lemon myrtle leaves.
3. To prepare the stuffing, mix together the garlic, onions, celery, carrots, lemon myrtle leaves and seasoning. Push the stuffing into the cavity of the bustard and then place it in the camp oven.
4. Place the camp oven on the coals and shovel more hot coals on top and around the camp oven.
5. Cook for approximately 35–45 minutes (for a small bustard, or 40–50 minutes if a large bustard), or until it's cooked through and the skin is a lovely golden brown.

Serve with roasted vegetables.

Native dukkah-crusted kangaroo steaks with Davidson's plum sauce

60 min

Serves 4

INGREDIENTS

Davidson's plum sauce

- ¾ cup water
- 300g caster sugar
- 1 cinnamon stick
- ¾ glass red wine
- 1 star anise
- 500g Davidson's plums, washed and quartered (no need to deseed)
- pinch of salt

RECIPES

Kangaroo

- 1 large purple yam or sweet potato, peeled and sliced
- 4 tablespoons olive oil
- 500g kangaroo fillets
- 8 broccolini stalks

Dukkah mix

See recipe for Native bush dukkah, page 162

METHOD

Davidson's plum sauce

1. In a saucepan, mix the water, sugar, cinnamon stick, wine and star anise. Bring to a boil.
2. Once the mixture has boiled and the sugar has dissolved, add the Davidson's plums and simmer on the lowest heat for about an hour until the plums have completely disintegrated.
3. Strain the sauce through a sieve, keeping the liquid. Discard the skins, seeds and any pulp. Put the liquid back into the saucepan and reduce by half until thickened.
4. Add salt to taste, stir then pour into a jug and cool to room temperature.

NOTE: The sauce is best prepared at least an hour before cooking, or even the day before. Store cooked sauce in a jar or airtight container; refrigerate until ready to use.

Kangaroo and purple yams

1. Pre-heat an oven to 180°C. Spread the yams or sweet potato over a tray and drizzle with 1 tablespoon of olive oil, place in the oven and cook for 10–15 minutes or until golden brown.
2. Prepare your dukkah as per the recipe. Season with salt to taste.
3. Place the kangaroo fillets onto a baking tray, pour over half the oil. Take the dry dukkah mix and sprinkle all over the minya (meat), ensuring each fillet is well coated.
4. Heat a large, non-stick frying pan over medium–high heat. Add the remaining oil and the kangaroo fillets to the pan and cook for 4–5 minutes each side or until cooked to your liking. **NOTE: Kangaroo is best cooked medium.**
5. Boil, steam, or microwave broccolini until tender. Place the cooked broccolini into a bowl and season with sea salt and cracked pepper. Toss to combine.
6. Cut the kangaroo fillets into thick slices and pour over the resting juices.

To serve, pour the sauce over the sliced kangaroo fillets. Serve with broccolini and purple yams on the side.

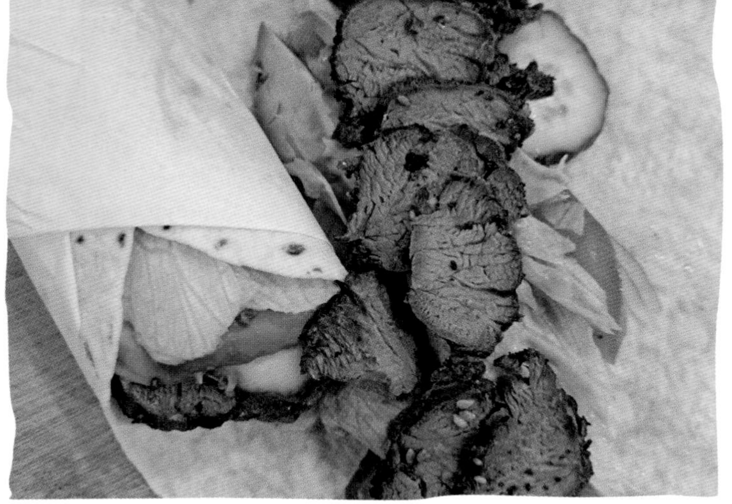

Kangaroo salad wraps

45 min

Serves 4

INGREDIENTS

Kangaroo and dry native herb crust

- ½ teaspoon each salt and pepper
- 2 tablespoons crushed lemon myrtle leaves
- 2 tablespoons crushed wattleseed
- 2 tablespoons sesame seeds
- 1 tablespoon turmeric
- 1 tablespoon roasted paprika
- 500g kangaroo fillets or steaks
- 4 tablespoons oil

Wrap and salad

- 1 avocado
- ½ lime
- 4 pita bread wraps
- 1 red onion, thinly sliced
- 1 tomato, thinly sliced
- 1 cucumber, thinly sliced
- 1/4 iceberg lettuce, thinly sliced
- 1 capsicum, thinly sliced
- 1 handful rocket
- 1 tablespoon egg mayonnaise

METHOD

1. Preheat the oven to 200°C or prepare an air fryer, as per the manufacturer's recommendations.
2. Peel and deseed the avocado and place in a bowl; squeeze the juice of the lime on top. Mash the avocado and lime juice together using a fork until roughly blended, set aside.
3. In a large mixing bowl, mix all the dry crust ingredients together. Add the kangaroo fillets and toss to cover generously.
4. Bring your frying pan up to heat and add the oil. Place the kangaroo fillets in the hot pan and leave for a few minutes until you see the colour changing. Turn evenly to ensure all sides are cooked well (this may take 10–15 minutes). Once all sides are seared through, turn the heat to medium and let them cook through for another 15 minutes. Set the fillets aside for a few minutes to rest.
5. Place the kangaroo onto a tray and transfer into the oven or air fryer for a further 10 minutes to finish cooking. Once it's finished, removed from the oven and let it rest well again.

6. Once the minya (meat) has rested, slice and divide it evenly into four to be added to the wraps.
7. Lay the wraps on a clean dry surface. Start with a thin layer of mayonnaise spread across the wrap, then add all your sliced vegetables, the smashed avocado and the minya. Keeping in mind that you will need to fold the wrap, it's best to not fill it with too many ingredients.
8. To fold your wraps, start with the bottom, then the sides. Once it's wrapped – sit back and enjoy.

Lemon myrtle kangaroo tail stew served on creamy mashed potatoes

3 hrs

Serves 4

INGREDIENTS

Lemon myrtle stew

- 4 tablespoons salted butter
- 1kg kangaroo tail (less if using a boneless cut)
- 1 onion, diced
- 1 garlic clove, crushed
- 2 tablespoons ginger, crushed or finely chopped
- 1 teaspoon paprika
- 4 tablespoons plain flour or corn flour for thickening
- 1 cup red wine or Worcestershire sauce, or a mix of both
- 400g can diced tomatoes

- 2 litres beef stock or water
- 3 lemon myrtle leaves, fresh or dried
- 1 tablespoon bush mix (pepper berries, saltbush, lemon myrtle)
- 4 carrots, chopped into large pieces
- 4 celery sticks, roughly chopped
- ½ kent pumpkin, largely chopped
- 400g can butter beans
- 4 tomatoes, roughly chopped

Mashed Potatoes

- 4 potatoes, peeled and roughly chopped
- 2 lemon myrtle leaves
- 1 pinch salt
- 4 garlic cloves
- 2 tablespoons butter
- 4 tablespoons cream or plain yogurt
- bush mix or salt and pepper for seasoning

METHOD

Kangaroo stew

1. Heat half the butter in a large pot. Season the kangaroo tails with salt and pepper and add to the pot to brown, remove once browned all over.
2. Add the remaining butter to the pot along with the onion, garlic, ginger and paprika. Add the flour and stir until all ingredients are soft and the flour and butter form a paste.
3. Poor in the red wine or Worcestershire sauce and bring to the boil. Once boiled, add the canned tomatoes, beef stock, lemon myrtle leaves and the bush mix and bring back to the boil.

4. Return the kangaroo tails to the pot of liquid and add more water or stock to ensure all the tails are covered, continue to cook on high for another 2 hours.
5. After 2 hours, check to see if the minya is starting to soften and reduce to a medium heat. Add the carrots, celery, pumpkin, butter beans and chopped tomatoes and stir well. Continue to cook on medium heat for another hour.

Mashed potatoes

1. Fill a medium-sized pot with water, add the lemon myrtle leaves, garlic cloves and a pinch of salt. Bring to the boil, then add the potatoes. Cook until the potatoes are soft.
2. Drain the water and return the potatoes to the pot, add the butter and start to mash using a potato masher or a fork.
3. Once the potato is mashed to a nice consistency, add the cream or yogurt and mix well. Season with the bush mix, or salt and pepper to taste.

To serve, place a bed of mash potato in a bowl, then spoon the kangaroo stew on top. Season if desired and serve with crusty bread or damper. The stew can also be served with rice.

NOTE: Other vegetables can be used in the stew such as zucchinis, potatoes, beans, sweet potatoes, capsicum, button mushrooms, brussels sprouts, cabbage, broccoli and peas. It's up to you to be adventurous.

Caramelised cluster figs and ice-cream

15 min

Serves 4–6

INGREDIENTS

- 5–10 cluster figs, washed, stems removed and halved
- 2 tablespoons salted butter
- 2 tablespoons brown sugar
- 1 lemon peel
- pinch of cinnamon powder

METHOD

1. Melt butter and brown sugar in a fry pan. Add lemon peel and cinnamon to create a sugar sauce.
2. Add the figs and cook for approximately 1–2 minutes or until figs turn a soft brown colour.

Serve with an ice-cream flavour of your choice.

Bush passionfruit and gooseberry fruit salad

10 min

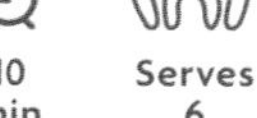
Serves 6

INGREDIENTS

- 2 bananas
- 1 orange
- 1 red apple
- 1 pear
- 2 kiwifruit
- 10–15 native gooseberries
- 10–20 bush passionfruits (careful not to squash them)

METHOD

1. Peel bananas and orange and cut into whatever size you prefer.
2. Cut the apple, pear and kiwifruit into whatever size you prefer.
3. Place all the cut fruit and the gooseberries in a large bowl and toss gently.
4. Add the passionfruit, whole, or squeeze the seeds over your salad and toss before serving.

You don't have to limit yourself to these ingredients. You can use whatever fruits are in season.

Traditional baked cheesecake with conkerberry and blueberry syrup

45 min

Serves 6

INGREDIENTS

Cheesecake

- 275g Anzac biscuits
- 70g butter, melted
- 4 tablespoons lemon myrtle powder
- 250g cream cheese
- 150g sour cream
- 75g caster sugar
- 2 eggs
- seeds from 1 vanilla bean, or 1½ teaspoons vanilla essence

Syrup

- 1 cup fresh conkerberries
- 1 cup fresh or frozen blueberries
- ¾ cup caster sugar
- ¼ cup water
- pinch of cinnamon
- ½ teaspoon vanilla essence

METHOD

Cheesecake

1. Preheat the oven to 190°C, and grease a 25cm springform cake tin well.
2. Add Anzac biscuits, lemon myrtle and melted butter to a food processor, and process until a smooth mixture forms. Spread the biscuit mixture evenly around the base of the cake tin, and press down on the mixture to ensure there are not gaps in the base. Cover the tin with cling wrap and place in the fridge.
3. In a mixing bowl, place the cream cheese, sour cream, caster sugar, eggs and vanilla essence. Mix well, until all ingredients are combined. For the best results, place the mixture into a food processor and process until it is smooth and creamy.
4. Take your base back out of the fridge and remove the cling wrap. Pour the cheese mixture on top of the biscuit base and spread evenly. Place the cheesecake into the oven and bake for 1 hour. When cooked, turn the oven off but leave the cheesecake in the oven with the door slightly ajar until it cools down; this will help prevent the cheesecake from cracking.

5. Once cooled, remove the cheesecake from the oven and place in the fridge for 4 hours, until chilled. Then remove the cheesecake from the cake tin.

Syrup

1. Put conkerberries, blueberries, caster sugar and water in a small saucepan over medium heat and bring to the boil, stirring gently at all times. Once boiling slightly, reduce heat.
2. Add cinnamon and vanilla essence to the syrup and stir gently until the syrup thickens. If the sauce is too thick, add water to thin it to your liking.
3. Once it reaches a syrup-like consistency, remove from heat. Allow syrup to cool to room temperature.

To serve, drizzle the berry syrup over the cheesecake.

Where to buy bush tukka

You can purchase bush tukka from the following websites:

Australian Bush Foods
Rainforest Bounty
www.rainforestbounty.com.au

Kimberley Wild Gubinge
www.kimberleywildgubinge.com.au

Kakadu Plum Co
www.kakaduplumco.com

Bindi Bindi Dreaming
www.bindibindidreaming.
com.au

My Dilly Bag
www.mydillybag.com.au

Bush tucker recipes
www.bushtuckerrecipes.com

Bush Tucker Shop
www.bushtuckershop.com

Indigiearth
www.indigiearth.com.au

Bush Food Pantry
www.bushfoodpantry.com.au

Tucker Bush
www.tuckerbush.com.au

Dreamtime Kullilla Art
www.kullillaart.com.au

Native Tastes of Australia
www.tasteaustralia.biz

Oz Tukka
www.oztukka.com.au

Taste Australia
www.bushfoodshop.com.au

Australian Native Food Co
www.australiannativefoodco.com.au

The Source Bulk Foods
www.thesourcebulkfoods.com.au

Where to buy bush tukka plants

Australian Plants online
www.australianplantsonline.com.au

Melbourne Bushfoods
www.melbournebushfood.com.au

Witjuti Grub Bushfood Nursery
www.witjutigrub.com.au

Yuruga Nursery
www.yuruga.com.au

Thank you ...

I would like to express my gratitude to Ella Woods, my amazing Editor, who worked tirelessly on this book. You made everything flow so well and helped keep me on track when everything felt so far away. Your passion for my book was very obvious and I want to thank you for your valuable expertise, advice and directions. You have been an absolute pleasure to work with!

I am extremely humbled and want to extend a special acknowledgement and thank you to the great team at Hardie Grant Explore, Melissa Kayser and Amanda Louey, as well as everyone behind the scenes. Thank you for giving me the opportunity to revitalise Bush Tukka Guide and give it a brand new and exciting makeover. Not only have you worked tirelessly in keeping me on track with my deadlines, you've been amazing to work with and have believed in me when, behind the scenes in my world, I did not think I could pull any of this off. You all have given me unconditional support and through this, I owe my humble confidence to you!

Thank you once again ladies!

Index

INDEX